The Building Blocks of Ear

Young children need to develop and understand the core basic concepts in mathematics before they can move forwards in their mathematical learning. Without these solid foundations, they are more likely to have gaps in their knowledge and require intervention in their primary years. This new book provides guidance and resources to help you develop children's key skills and understanding in mathematics.

Written by experienced teachers, the book outlines key mathematical concepts and provides a wide range of exciting, mathematically rich activities that support the development of these concepts. It exposes some of the common misconceptions and errors that practitioners may observe children showing in their settings and offers simple, practical strategies to help move children forwards in their thinking and understanding.

Covering all areas of mathematics learning – counting and number, calculation, shape and space, pattern, measuring and handling data – the book features:

- practical ideas for supporting assessment, observation, mathematical vocabulary and building links with home;
- activities that promote a child-led approach, linked to children's everyday lives and experiences;
- guidance on how to extend and challenge children's learning through adult-led, quality teaching and effective practice;
- a clear sense of progression based on children's understanding rather than age.

Written by experienced practitioners, *The Building Blocks of Early Maths* will help you to ensure that the children in your care have the strong foundations they need to become confident, successful mathematicians in the future.

Elaine Bennett is an Early Years and Maths Specialist currently based at Friars Primary School and Nursery in Southend. She also works as Early Years Advisor at Southend Local Authority supporting settings across the borough and advising on best practice.

Jenny Weidner is a Senior Teacher at Earls Hall Infant School. She has also advised on best practice within Southend Local Authority as an Advanced Skills Teacher, specialising in Mathematics and Foundation Stage/Key Stage 1.

The Building Blocks of Early Maths

Bringing key concepts to life
for 3–6 year olds

Elaine Bennett
and
Jenny Weidner

Routledge
Taylor & Francis Group

LONDON AND NEW YORK

First published 2014
by Routledge
2 Park Square, Milton Park, Abingdon, Oxon OX14 4RN

and by Routledge
711 Third Avenue, New York, NY 10017

Routledge is an imprint of the Taylor & Francis Group, an informa business

British Library Cataloguing in Publication Data
A catalogue record for this book is available from the British Library

Library of Congress Cataloging in Publication Data
Bennett, Elaine.
The building blocks of early maths : bringing key concepts to life for 3-6 year olds / Elaine Bennett and Jenny Weidner.
pages cm
1. Mathematics--Study and teaching (Preschool) 2. Mathematics--Study and teaching (Early childhood) I. Weidner, Jenny. II. Title. III. Title: Building blocks of early math.
QA135.6.B4673 2014
372.7'049--dc23
2013044451

ISBN: 978-0-415-65739-6 (hbk)
ISBN: 978-0-415-65740-2 (pbk)
ISBN: 978-0-203-07697-2 (ebk)

Typeset in Optima
by Saxon Graphics Ltd, Derby

Printed and bound by CPI Group (UK) Ltd, Croydon, CR0 4YY

Contents

Acknowledgements

We would like to thank Annamarie at Routledge for inspiring us to write this book and her vision for how to further support practitioners in bringing maths to life for young children.

A very special thank you goes to our amazing families who continue to provide the love and support that enable us to follow our ambitions. And a final thank you to Luca and Maxwell, we love every second of watching you both grow and learn and we cannot wait to share your wonderful learning journeys that are only just beginning!

Introduction

Maths is all around us

Children are born into a world rich in mathematics and begin developing their own ideas about mathematics from an early age through play and exploration. The type of mathematical connections and experiences children encounter in these early stages such as when fitting wooden bricks into a push along trolley, or exploring pouring and filling teapots with water are born from a child's natural desire to learn and curiosity to find out about the world around them. Even a very young child can be observed persevering with these types of activities, or seen returning to repeat these time and time again. This is because they are in control of these activities and each time they repeat it their learning and thinking moves forwards, often without the need for adult intervention. As children grow and move into more formal learning environments maths can become something different, where activities are adult directed and time and space may not allow for such child led opportunities. Just like the child that prefers the box rather than the present at Christmas, how many times do practitioners set up activities they think will interest the children, yet they are left untouched.

Figure 0.1 Even from a young age, children demonstrate their ability to find and solve their own problems.

Meaningful maths

Children grow up experiencing maths in everyday life, perhaps as a baby an adult may count their toes, with a toddler they may count the steps they can climb and with an older child it may be the number of buttons on their coat. These types of simple, everyday experiences are helping children to learn about maths in a relevant and personal way. Maths is important for young children and throughout their day in their learning environment they will encounter many problems that need solving, such as fitting books into the book box, counting pencils into pots, making sure there is enough water in the jug for drinks at snack time and helping the practitioner work out whose lunchbox is missing from the trolley. In these early days of education maths is purposeful and needed. So what is it that happens as children get older that maths becomes irrelevant and impersonal, for example working out how many slabs are needed to build a patio, or the time an imaginary train arrives at an imaginary station?

For some children maths becomes a subject in which they lose confidence and see themselves as failures. Learning in maths is based upon core concepts and understanding. As children progress through school those who do not have a secure understanding of the basic building blocks of maths, i.e. key concepts, will struggle to make progress. When practitioners do not recognise the underlying problems or misconceptions for children who are struggling with maths, intervention is often pitched too high when a back to basics approach is needed. This book aims to identify the core building blocks of maths that young children need to understand to prepare them for the mathematical learning journey that lies ahead of them.

Building blocks of maths

Maths is such a diverse subject, covering topics such as number, time, capacity, shape, money, calculating and length. Within these topics children will show different areas of strength and ability. It is quite easy to say whether a child is good at reading or not, however within maths they could excel at number and calculating but struggle to tell the time, or they may show excellent spatial awareness and understanding of position but struggle to add and subtract. Within the many aspects of maths there are building blocks, i.e. key concepts that children need to understand and be secure with in order to become confident, able mathematicians, not just in school, but in real life.

How to use this book

The common thread running through this book relates to building. Maths is like a building, made up of many bricks, which connect together and form a strong structure. When working with young children the practitioner needs to ensure that the environment and opportunities on offer help children to set the foundations on which this building will stand. They will continue building and adding to this structure throughout school and into adult life. Without the firmest foundations at the bottom this structure will crumble, in other words there will be gaps in their mathematical understanding.

This book consists of five main chapters outlining the main areas of maths: Counting and number, Measuring, Data handling, Calculating and Shape and space. The sixth chapter considers how to support links with parents/carers to ensure children experience meaningful mathematics at home.

Each of the main chapters follows the same format and consists of:

- Introduction: An outline of the focus area of maths.
- Everyday experiences: A list of children's everyday experiences for practitioners to build on and consider.
- The building blocks: A summary of the key concepts within the area of maths.
- Key vocabulary (taken from the *Mathematical Vocabulary Book*, National Strategies 2008): A list of useful words to use when working with children and to promote within the learning environment. It is more a guide for practitioners than a checklist of words that children must say.

- Moving on: Three clear stages of progression. This summarises what practitioners would expect from children ranging from three to six years old. The stages are not referred to as age related expectations, instead three progressive stages linked to children's developing mathematical understanding: laying the foundations (broadly in line with 22–36 and 30–50 month age bands as set out in *Development Matters in the Early Years Foundation Stage (EYFS),* Early Education 2012 and *Early Years Outcomes* Department for Education 2013); beginning to build (broadly in line with 40–60+ month age band); and building up (broadly in line with Year 1 expectations as set out in the *National Curriculum,* Dfe 2013 and Primary Framework, DfES 2006). These broad stages will enable practitioners to see where children are in all key areas of maths and to plan for their next steps.

- Building together: 12 main activities based on the building blocks of the focus area of maths. There are four themes within each area and activities relating to the three stages of progression (outlined above). These are adult led activities largely aimed at small groups to help children to secure understanding of the key concepts and provide opportunities to make the activity easier (for a child working at an earlier stage) and harder (for a child working beyond this stage).

- Assessment and observation: This provides simple prompts for practitioners to consider when observing and working with children in the focus area.

- Stumbling blocks: An outline of possible difficulties or misconceptions children may have in this area of mathematics. There are suggestions for simple ways to support children in overcoming these barriers to learning. It is vital to make a 'maths-safe' environment, where mistakes and misconceptions are embraced and used as a learning tool. Children need to see adults making mistakes to understand that this is acceptable, and proof that true learning is happening. If no child makes a mistake, has the practitioner pitched their learning with enough challenge?

- Useful tools: A simple list of resources that could be used when working both inside and out. These are not merely for adult led activities, but for children to initiate their own learning.

- Stories and rhymes: Suggestions for stories and rhymes to use to inspire learning within this area of maths.

We hope that this book will provide you with insight into the crucial mathematical learning and experiences that children need to develop and explore in their early years in order to grow into confident and independent mathematicians. This book will help you to realise what children need to know and understand and how you as a practitioner can ensure this learning happens! The simple adult led, playful activities will support you as you work with children to start them on their mathematical learning journey, providing the experiences that ensure they are developing not only the key concepts and skills they need in order to succeed, but also a positive, can do approach to all things mathematical. We hope that the chapters inspire you to plan and deliver exciting activities to match your children's needs, interests and fascinations, whether they are 'laying the foundations', 'beginning to build' or 'building up'.

1 Counting and number

Introduction

Children are surrounded by numbers and this is perhaps the area of maths that children are exposed to from the youngest age. From counting stairs, hearing number rhymes, listening to favourite traditional stories and being out and about whether shopping or at the park. These types of real life experiences can all go some way towards developing a true sense of number and counting. The reason these experiences are so valuable is because they are meaningful and are relevant to children's lives. They also enable children to begin to make connections, for example the meaning of the number three could be their age, the number of billy goats in a story, how many plates are on their dinner table or the number on their front door. As practitioners working with young children we have lost count of the number of times that children will see a number and excitedly exclaim 'That's how old I am!' or 'That's the number on my nanny's door!' This clearly demonstrates how children want numbers to be personal to them and are continually searching to make sense of the numbers around them and the connections between them. As children progress through their education a solid sense of number and counting is crucial in order for them to calculate, compare quantities and solve problems. Where children do not have this solid understanding they are simply following mathematical rules or processes without truly understanding them.

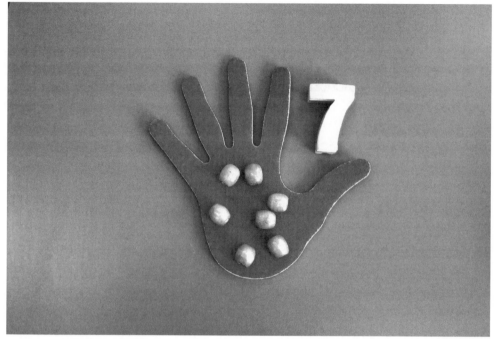

Figure 1.1 Provide interesting and unusual objects to spark children's interest in counting.

Everyday experiences of number and counting

- Comparing scores on computer games
- Door numbers
- Television channels
- Ages
- Telephone numbers
- Bus numbers
- Games and jigsaws
- Getting dressed
- Shopping
- Cooking

What are the building blocks?

How many? (Cardinal)

This is about children being able to accurately count objects, knowing that the last number said is the number of objects in the group and that each object is only counted once. They need to understand that it does not affect the total if the group is rearranged or counted in a different order.

Counting out loud

This is about children understanding that when we count aloud there is a set order for the number names, beginning one, two, three, four, five. Even as children begin to count in steps of two, five or ten they are using their knowledge of this number order.

Ordinal

This is about using numbers to describe the place or position of a person or object, for example you would not say someone was three in the line, you would say they were third in the line.

Estimation

This is about using children's sense of number to make sensible and accurate guesses about quantities and amounts and recognising that an estimate does not need to be exact. Children are often reluctant to make a guess that may not be correct, when in fact a near guess is an essential tool in life, such as checking change in a shop or working out costs.

Place value

This is about the place and value of digits within the number system and, as numbers get bigger, what each digit represents such as ones, tens or hundreds. A solid grasp of place value is essential for the development of calculation skills and for children understanding what is happening to numbers as they add, subtract, multiply and divide.

Reading and writing numbers

This is about children being able to recognise and record numerals to represent amounts such as how many objects in a box, quantities such as how long something is and labels such as a number on a door.

Key vocabulary

- Number
- Zero, one, two, three…
- How many?
- Count up to
- Count on
- Count back
- More
- Less
- Odd
- Even
- Estimate
- Near
- Fewer
- Bigger
- Compare
- First, second, third…
- Before
- After
- Next
- Units, ones
- Tens
- Teens

Moving on:
What does it look like at the three stages of progression?

Laying the foundations
Children at this stage:

- use numbers in their play;
- use developing mathematical language in everyday contexts;
- will probably be able to count up to 10 orally;
- may be beginning to try and record numbers by making marks or showing numbers on their fingers;
- enjoy joining in with counting activities such as counting toys, singing songs, etc.

Beginning to build
Children at this stage:

- count up to 20 orally and can order numbers up to 10, then 20;
- make simple estimates of how many objects are in a group and check by counting;
- say one more and one less than a given number to 10 and beyond;
- record numbers with increasing accuracy in play activities.

Building up
Children at this stage:

- count at least 20 objects accurately;
- begin to count to and across 100, forwards and backwards, beginning with 0 or 1, or from any given number;
- learn to count, read and write numbers to 100 in numerals; initially to 20, with a focus on teens numbers;
- identify and represent numbers using objects and pictures including the number line;
- compare and order numbers using the language of: equal to, more than, less than (fewer), most, least;
- begin to understand what each digit in a number represents, starting with teen numbers;
- say the number that is one more or less and ten more or less than a multiple of ten;
- recognise sequences and patterns, including odd and even numbers.

Building together

Matching game

Building blocks:

- How many
- Counting out loud
- Reading and writing numbers

Moving on:

Laying the foundations

You will need:

Buckets or bags, sticky labels, washing line, natural 'treasures' available in the outdoor area such as coloured leaves, stones, pebbles, sticks, twigs, fir cones, conkers, acorns

Main activity:

Talk to the children about the 'treasures' they could find in the outdoor area such as colourful leaves, stones, fir cones, twigs, etc. Hang a selection of buckets or bags on a washing line or wall. Explain to the children that each bucket or bag can only hold a certain number of treasures. Get the children to help you label the buckets or bags using marks, numerals or dots up to five or ten depending on the children's abilities. Look at the labels on the buckets together and count out loud together until you get to the number that is on the label. Using a range of natural treasures demonstrate how to put the correct number of objects in the bucket. For example, if it is labelled with the number three, then count out loud one count every time you pick up an object until you get to three. Then check by touching each object and counting again. Put the treasures in the bucket. Allow children time to search for and collect a range of treasures and then observe as they count and place them in the buckets. Remind the children to count aloud as they select their objects or to touch each object they have as they count aloud before putting them into the bucket. Once each bucket has treasure inside it gather the children together and check that each bucket has the correct number of objects inside it. Begin by asking the children 'How many treasures are meant to be in the bucket?' then check by counting aloud together with the practitioner modelling touching each object, then once the last object has been counted ask again 'How many treasures do we have?' Model to the children that the last count represents the number of treasures they have. Children could then repeat the task but labelling the buckets themselves.

Make it easier: Only label buckets with up to three items or provide simple picture cards with two leaves, three stones, one stick, etc. drawn on it so that children can match the objects they find to the cards. Practice counting aloud with the children as they find the objects.

Make it harder: Instead of labelling the buckets with numbers provide each child with a bucket. Explain that they are going to hunt for natural treasures and can fill their buckets but they must only pick one type of natural treasure to collect, such as only leaves or stones. Each child takes their bucket to fill and then returns to the group. Children then respond to the question 'How many treasures do you think are in your bucket?' by estimating. Ask the children how they could check whether they are correct. Count the objects together, encouraging the children to count aloud with you, ensuring that they only count each object as it is taken from the bucket.

Out and about

Scavenger hunt
Building blocks:

- How many
- Counting out loud
- Reading and writing numbers

Moving on:

Beginning to build

You will need:

Paper or plastic bags, sticky labels, felt tips/crayons/pencils, sand timer, natural objects such as stones, leaves, pebbles or sticks available in the outdoor area, pegs, washing line

Main activity:

Provide children with paper bags or plastic bags and sticky labels. Explain that they are going to be working together to create their own outdoor number line. Count from one to ten aloud with the children and then line them up in a row and repeat the count with each child saying one number. Using felt tips, pencils or crayons children then label their bag with the number of items they need to find (the same number that they said aloud in the oral count along the row of children). If there are more than ten children make two smaller number lines rather than continuing beyond ten. Once their bags are labelled using marks, dots or numerals ask each child to count aloud from one to their given number. The practitioner then emphasises that this is how many objects they will be searching for in the scavenger hunt. Use a minute or three minute timer and set the challenge that children need to find the correct number of natural objects to put into their bag within the time. Once the children have collected their objects ask them to return to the groups and place their items within their bags. How many objects does each child have in their bag? How can they check whether they do have the correct number? Count aloud with the child as they point to each of their objects to ensure they have the right amount. Children then hold their bags and arrange themselves into the correct order, starting with the child holding the number one bag. Count along the line to ensure they are in the correct order with either the practitioner counting aloud with the children or each child saying their number one after the other. Children then peg their bags on a washing line outside to make an outdoor number line. The bags can then be emptied and children can fill the bags with the correct number of objects when playing or working outside.

Make it easier: Create a number line up to five and instead of using numerals label the bags with pictures of the objects to collect and dots in the patterns they have seen on dice to support their counting.

Make it harder: Create a number line that is from 1 to 20. Can the children count aloud to 20? Can they count back from 20 using the outdoor number line? Ensure children count aloud when counting their objects so that the practitioner can note any mispronounced words such as saying 'ty' for 'teen'.

Out and about

Counting by grouping

Building blocks:

- How many
- Counting out loud

Moving on:

Building up

You will need:

Boxes, bags, pots, buckets, natural objects available in the outdoor area such as leaves, twigs, stones, pebbles, fir cones, acorns, conkers, pencils, sticky notes

Main activity:

Provide children with a range of boxes, bags, pots and buckets and explain that they are to search the outdoor area for natural objects to fill their container but they must decide on only one type of object to collect, such as pebbles or leaves. Give them time to search for and collect the objects to fill their containers. Once the children have finished collecting, gather them together again and ask them how many objects they think they have in their container. Can they make a sensible estimate by looking at the contents of their container? What will be the best way to count their objects to check if their guess was right? Practise counting out loud as a group for numbers to 20 and beyond. Can they count using any patterns apart from ones? How about in twos or tens? Practise counting aloud in twos and tens together. Give children time to count their objects, and prompt the use of strategies that were suggested by the children. Discuss how children chose to count the contents of their container. Did anyone count them in ones? Ask them to demonstrate this to the other children, is this a quick way of counting? Did any other children choose a different way to count? Demonstrate their suggestions and talk about whether these ways are any quicker than counting in ones. Show children how to group the objects to enable them to count the objects quickly, start with putting them into groups of two for numbers up to 20 and tens for numbers larger than 20. How does grouping help to count the objects? Is it quicker than counting every object? Allow children to then re-count their objects using grouping. Was their estimate accurate? Children can then practise grouping their objects in different ways but ensure they understand that the total of the objects remains the same no matter how they are grouped.

Make it easier: Demonstrate how to count objects effectively in ones by placing them in a row or by moving each object each time they say a number. Ensure counting aloud is done together to model one-to-one correspondence and to make sure they understand that the last count they make is the total of the objects they have.

Make it harder: Encourage children to also group in fives and then possibly threes, if they can count aloud in these patterns. Talk about the importance of choosing how they group the objects by looking at the quantity, for example it would be quicker to count in tens than twos with a large quantity but more effective to count a smaller number of objects in twos.

Puzzles and games

Collecting game

Building blocks:

- Ordinal numbers
- Reading and writing numbers

Moving on:

Laying the foundations

You will need:

A 'one, one, two, two, three, three' dice, bowls or pots to collect in, interesting objects to collect, e.g. shells, glass pebbles, shiny objects, some first, second, third, fourth, fifth, sixth badges, rosettes or medals made by the children to award as prizes for each player

Main activity:

Children take it in turns to roll the dice and choose from the interesting objects to put into their pots. After each turn practice counting how many things there are altogether. Children could find or record the matching numeral after each turn.

After a few rolls, put each person's objects in a row along with the numeral to show the total and talk about who has the longest row to decide who gets the first prize. Then remove this row and ask whose row is the next longest to get second prize and do the same for third, fourth and fifth (or as many players as are in the group).

Make it easier: Use a large dice and build up a set of objects together as a group, with each person taking a turn to roll and collect the objects. After each roll the matching numeral could be modelled by an adult.

Make it harder: Children play individually. Use a one-to-six dice and devise a simple chart with first, second, third, fourth, fifth (or as many rolls as each child will get) down the side with a space next to it. As children roll the dice after each roll they record how many they have in their collection on their chart. Repeat this after the second, third, fourth roll and so on. At the end of the game ask questions such as 'How many did you have after your first roll', 'Who had the most objects after their third roll?' and so on. This supports data handling work too.

Puzzles and games

Skittles

Building blocks:

- Ordinal numbers
- Reading and writing numbers

Moving on:

Beginning to build

You will need:

Empty bottles or cardboard tubes to make skittles from, a large soft ball, paper to make labels for the skittles, clipboards, paper and pens for score keeping

Main activity:

Make skittles with the children using recycled materials. Plastic bottles could be used with some sand inside to make them harder to knock over. This could link to learning about the world and children could investigate how much sand is needed to allow the bottle to stand upright yet be able to be knocked down. Alternatively cardboard tubes (such as kitchen roll inserts) could be used, although, if working outside these blow away more easily. Decide with the children how many skittles need to be made and provide creative materials for them to decorate them with as well as some labels for numbers to be recorded onto to be fixed onto the skittles. Once the skittles have been made children can investigate the best way to arrange them for playing skittles and take it in turns to roll the ball and knock some over. The total number of skittles knocked down by each player could be recorded, or alternatively the numbers on the skittles knocked down could be circled on a number line or track. At the end of the game children could be ordered according to how many they knocked down and badges/medals they have made for first, second, third, fourth, fifth, sixth awarded.

Make it easier: Children roll the ball at fewer skittles, perhaps a set of five, counting how many are knocked down each time and holding up the appropriate numeral card to match how many were knocked down. As each player queues to have a turn, language such as 'It's your turn first', 'You are second' and 'It's your turn third' could be reinforced.

Make it harder: Children could have three rolls each and talk about which numbered skittles are knocked down after the first, second, third roll. A child (or adult) with a clipboard could record the numbers of the skittles which were knocked down each time. Scores could be compared by adding the totals of skittles knocked down and circling the total on a number line. Children could be ordered according to how many points were achieved and medals/rosettes awarded (e.g. first, second, third, fourth).

Puzzles and games

Track games

Building blocks:

- Ordinal numbers
- Reading and writing numbers

Moving on:

Building up

You will need:

Prepare paper (A4 size or larger), each piece with a blank number track drawn on, try to ensure these do not all go straight across the page but go in different pathways (e.g. winding, spiral, curved and circular), number tiles or cards, dice, counters, mark making materials

Main activity:

This is a simple and versatile activity that could be linked to most themes, topics or favourite stories. Children invent their own track game by numbering the squares on a track (using the number tiles or cards if needed to remind them of formation) and thinking of instructions to go onto some of the squares such as 'miss a go', 'go forwards three', 'go back two' and so on. Children could also think of questions that have to be answered if special spaces are landed on (perhaps spaces with a star or question mark). These could be maths questions or linked to current learning. Reinforce ordinal language as children play the game and challenge the children to make badges, medals or stickers to show the final position of players (first, second, third, fourth).

Make it easier: Use number tiles for children to make their own tracks outside or in a large space. Children roll the dice and physically travel around the track. Award medals to players in the order that they reach the end of the game. Add simple instructions such as 'move forwards one' and 'move back one' on special squares!

Make it harder: Using their paper track game as a plan, children recreate this on a large scale, making their own signs and captions for the game. Again medals can be awarded to players as they finish to show their finishing positions. The questions asked as they land on special spaces could be differentiated.

Bodies

Action game
Building blocks:

- Estimation
- Counting out loud

Moving on:

Laying the foundations

You will need:

A large one-to-six numbered dice, a dice with actions on each side: clap, stamp, nod, jump, blink, etc.

Main activity:

The basis of estimation is counting, so focus on matching movements to numbers with young children. Roll the dice and count the spots. Then roll the action dice. As a group perform the actions together counting aloud. Alternatively tell the children that you will clap and they have to say stop after a given number, e.g. five. Can they stop you at the right time if you do not count aloud to help them?

Make it easier: Use a 'one, one, two, two, three, three' dice and roll it to find out how many claps to do together. Focus on counting aloud, matching claps to numbers. Simple games where you drop objects into a tin and ask the children to stop you at a set point, also reinforce counting skills, as well as concentration!

Make it harder: Use a stop watch or timer. Children roll the action dice and estimate how many times they can do that action in a set number of seconds, such as five or ten. Can they find a way to record how many claps, stamps, blinks, jumps or nods they could do in the set time? What could they do most/ least of in the time? Circle the amount they estimate on a number line and then circle the actual number they could do. Was their estimate a good guess? How near/far were they from the actual amount? Repeat the activity to see if with practice their estimates improve. Remember to reinforce that estimating is good guessing… not necessarily the exact answer!

Bodies

Handfuls

Building blocks:

- Estimation

Moving on:

Beginning to build

You will need:

Outlines of hands, cut out and laminated, a basket of small objects, such as sorting toys, numerals, number track

Main activity:

Challenge the children to estimate how many of the small objects they could grab in one hand. Circle their estimates on a number line or track. Each child puts their hand into the pot and grabs a handful of objects then puts them on the hand cut-out in a pile. Encourage them to estimate again… do they want to change their estimate? Do they think it is more or less? Encourage them to count to check. Circle their estimate and then the amount on the number track. How close were they?

Make it easier: Use larger objects so that the children are not able to grab quite so many to focus on counting smaller groups of objects.

Make it harder: Add a challenge to the task for children to investigate. Who can hold the most objects in the class/school/their family? How many objects can you grab with two hands? What was the difference between the estimate and the final amount? Can you work this out on a number line or track?

Bodies

Wrap it

Building blocks:

- Estimation

Moving on:

Building up

You will need:

Wrapping paper with pictures on it or patterned napkins

Main activity:

Show the children a section of pictures on some wrapping paper (favourite current characters will grab their interest) or a patterned napkin. Flash this to them quickly so they do not have time to count and ask them to estimate how many pictures are on it (make sure this amount corresponds with their counting skills). Ask them to record their estimate (either on a whiteboard or a number line or track). Ask them to collect the matching number of buttons/interlocking cubes to match their estimate. Lay the paper in front of them and ask them to look at the group of objects they collected to match their estimate. Do the amounts look the same? Model matching the counted objects to the printed pictures by putting one object on each picture (reinforcing 1:1 correspondence). As they do this talk about whether they think they will have enough cubes/buttons to cover each picture... what does it tell them about their estimate if there are too many buttons or not enough? Look at how many buttons they have left over or are short by and record the total of printed pictures either on the whiteboard or number line and compare with their estimate. How close were they?

Make it easier: Use rubber spots or carpet mats to play musical chairs type games where they have to jump onto a mat or spot when the music stops. Will there be enough mats or spots for us all? When the music stops how many people are left out without a mat each time? How many more mats would be needed?

Make it harder: Work with estimating larger groups of objects and challenge children to work out how near or far their estimate was by counting on or back mentally.

Homes

Door numbers

Building blocks:

- Place value
- Reading and writing numbers

Moving on:

Laying the foundations

You will need:

Junk modelling boxes, paint, scissors, paper, felt tips/crayons/pencils, sticky labels, camera, black paper or wooden/plastic roadway pieces

Main activity:

Take the children on a walk around the local area and look carefully at the houses in their local streets. How does the postman know where each house is? Talk about the importance of having door numbers on the houses. Do any children know the number that they live at? Take photos of some of the houses and house numbers that they have seen to use in the setting. Once back inside, provide children with a range of different shaped and sized junk modelling boxes. Use black paper or plastic/wooden roadway pieces to create a road. Explain to the children that the houses on the street are missing so could they make some using the junk modelling resources. Remind them of the houses and house numbers they saw on their walk by looking at and talking about the photos that were taken. Allow them to paint and decorate their boxes to make them look like houses, talking about the features they have chosen and whether they are similar or different to their friend's house. Give the children sticky labels, felt tips, crayons or pencils and talk about how they could label their house with a number. Allow children to use marks or numerals to label their house. Talk about the number they have attached to their house and why, for example is it a number that is significant to them or the number of their own house? Model how to record these numerals for the children to attach next to their houses. Children then create their own street by placing the houses along the side of the road and can then use these for play. Labels with dots, marks or numerals for numbers one to five could also be placed on houses for the street to encourage children to play with and talk about these numbers and children or practitioners could model how to put these numbers in order.

Make it easier: If children are unable to record marks or numerals to represent numbers ask them to show their number on their fingers and take a photo. The practitioner could then record it for the child. A small version of the photo could also be attached to the house.

Make it harder: Challenge the children to make a street numbered from one to five, then one to ten. Can they label the houses using numerals or marks for each number and then put them in the correct order?

 Homes

Door number jumble

Building blocks:

- Place value
- Reading and writing numbers

Moving on:

Beginning to build

You will need:

Building blocks or boxes, sticky labels, number lines

Main activity:

Explain that the postman is trying to deliver letters to a street but he has a problem, the house numbers on the houses have all been stolen so he does not know where to deliver the letters. Provide children with building blocks or boxes set up in a street but without any labels on. Can the children create a street of houses with numbers in the correct order? The postman's road start at number one and finishes at ten/ twenty (depending on children's abilities). Can they make labels for the houses so that the postman knows where to deliver the letters? Give children time to label the houses and then arrange them in order to create a street from one to ten/twenty.

They can then check their work by counting aloud along the street and using a number line to compare their numbering. Once the street is complete explain that someone keeps mixing the numbers up and can they help to solve the problem? Ask children to close their eyes, swap two of the houses around and then children open their eyes and try to spot which houses have been mixed up. Can they put them back in the correct order? How did they know they were in the wrong place? Encourage them to talk about the order the houses should be in when you count aloud and where the mixed up houses were, such as 'between five and seven' or 'after eight'. Repeat this and challenge children by removing one or more houses from the street; can they decide which are missing and explain how they know? Relate this to one more or less than numbers to ten or twenty. Encourage children to count aloud and identify where they miscount because the house is missing.

Make it easier: Ask children to make a street from one to five, then progressing to six, then seven, etc. until they can order numbers to ten.

Make it harder: Introduce the concept of odd and even by creating a street using the houses numbered from one to twenty. Demonstrate this by placing house number one on one side of the road, then house number two on the other side and so on. What do the children notice about the numbers on the even side of the road? Count in twos with the children as they follow their finger along the houses along the even side of the road.

Homes

Ten street

Building blocks:

- Place value
- Reading and writing numbers

Moving on:

Building up

You will need:

Large paper, felt tips, pencils, wooden blocks or boxes, labels, straws, cubes, number squares

Main activity:

Explain that the local sorting office and postman have a problem. They have received lots of letters for different streets but do not know where the houses are on these streets. The name of the first street is Ten Street, which consists of houses that are numbered in multiples of tens. Can the children work in small teams to create a map of Ten Street for the postman to use to find the houses in the correct order? Ensure children are distinguishing between 'teen' and 'ty' numbers when they record them. Once they have made maps provide them with building blocks or boxes for them to label to create a model of Ten Street. Talk about the order of the numbers on Ten Street using questions such as 'What house would come after number 30?' or 'What number house would come between numbers 60 and 80?' Challenge children by removing one or more houses from the street; can they decide which are missing and explain how they know? Relate this to ten more or less than tens numbers to one hundred. Encourage children to count aloud and identify where they miscount because the house is missing.

This activity can then be repeated with other streets such as Two Street or Five Street. Can the children make maps of these streets? Again provide wooden blocks and labels to make models of the streets. Are any numbers in two of the streets? Are any numbers in all of the streets?

Make it easier: Repeat the same activity but explain that the street is Teen Street, where the numbers are from 10 to 20. Focus on what makes a 'teen' number by demonstrating that they are ten add one, ten add two, ten add three, etc. using models such as bundles of straws or towers of cubes. When making labels for the houses children could use marks such as lines and dots to represent the ten and ones that make up the number as well as writing the numeral.

Make it harder: Continue children's work on counting on and back in tens but instead of using tens numbers on Ten Street explain that the street begins on number 11. Each house in the street is ten more than the last. Can the children make a new map for this street and a model of the street, labelling the houses by counting aloud in tens from two-digit numbers? Encourage children to identify the next number by talking about how many tens and ones the previous number had. Children could also use a number square to support counting on in tens. Discuss the pattern of the numbers in the street with the tens increasing by one each time. Challenge children further by posing questions such as 'What if the road ended with the number 97; what would the first house be in the street?'

Assessment and observation

- Do they join in with counting activities?
- Can they recite number names in order?
- What strategies do they use to count objects, e.g. touching them, pointing to them, moving them, saying number names as they move them, etc.
- Can they order numbers? Can they talk about which numbers come before and after and how they know?
- How do they record numbers or their thinking about numbers and counting, e.g. pictures, tallies, etc.?
- What numbers do they recognise?

Stumbling blocks

The child says more than one number name per object resulting in an incorrect count.

- Model counting small groups of objects, saying the number as the object is moved and reinforcing that the last number said is the total.
- Use actions such as jumping, clapping, stamping or throwing beanbags with counting aloud.
- Count friends by touching each child on the head gently. Each child sits down when touched.
- Number rhymes with puppets or fingers, moving one at a time during the rhyme such as one finger hiding every time a duck swims away.

The child says 50 for 15, 30 for 13 when counting aloud.

- Use clear pronunciation and actions for 'ty' numbers such as drinking a cup of tea when a tens number is said when counting aloud. Make sure 'teen' numbers have a strong 'n' at the end when said aloud in any context.
- Use number lines or number cards to highlight the difference between 'ty' and 'teen', for example showing the child both numbers and asking which they meant to say; three tens or one ten and three ones.
- Using every opportunity to count aloud together, modelling correct language accompanied by the image such as a number line or number square.
- Use a range of models and images such as bead strings, arrow cards, bundles of straws to demonstrate the difference between tens and teen numbers.

The child counts an assortment of objects in an irregular arrangement by counting aloud but not stopping once all the objects have been counted resulting in re-counting some objects.

- Model strategies to count objects such as putting them in a line before counting or moving them aside to ensure they are not counted more than once.
- Use every opportunity to count objects in irregular arrangements (not in lines, and some things that cannot be moved or touched) to reinforce strategies, such as children on the carpet, trees in an outdoor area, lights on the ceiling. Begin with small numbers of objects and progress to larger amounts.

The child is reluctant to make estimates for fear of getting the answer wrong. Or a child makes estimates into the hundreds and thousands.

- Model estimating in everyday life such as fruit in a bowl, books in a box, children playing in an outdoor area, how many packed lunches and hot dinners for lunch. Demonstrate how to check the estimate and find out how close they were by looking on a number line.
- Practitioners to model estimating where they are unsure of the number to show children that estimates do not need to be exact to be a good guess.
- Provide opportunities in play for estimating and encourage children to 'have a go' and not be afraid to make a guess.

⚒ Useful tools

Small counting objects (caution to be taken with small children handling small objects)
Empty chocolate boxes
Pots
Tubs
Interesting boxes
Gift bags
Number lines
Number cards
Wrapping paper with patterns
Chalks
Pens
Clipboards
Dice
Washing lines and pegs

Simple board or track games
Puzzles
Clothes
Number rhyme puppets and props

📖 Stories and rhymes

Stories

The Teddy Bear Robber by Ian Beck, 2006, Picture Corgi.
Harry and the Bucketful of Dinosaurs by Ian Whybrow and Adrian Reynolds, 2008, Puffin.
The Jolly Postman by Janet and Allan Ahlberg, 1999, Puffin.
Goldilocks and the Three Bears.
Three Billy Goats Gruff.
Three Little Pigs.

Rhymes

'Five little ducks'
'Five little men in a flying saucer'
'One, two, three, four, five, once I caught a fish alive'
'One, two buckle my shoe'

2 Measuring

Introduction

From very early on in children's lives they develop ideas linked to measuring: that something is too heavy for them to pick up, that a toy will not fit in a box or what always happens after bath time. They therefore bring their own ideas, and possibly misconceptions, that they have developed through playing and exploring the world around them when they set foot within a more formal learning environment. Measuring is a practical area of mathematics that must be learnt through hands on, meaningful tasks. A child will only understand what 'heavy' means by lifting boxes of toys, logs or bricks, and how much containers can hold by pouring water into them until they overflow. The role of the practitioner is therefore key, to observe what the children are doing and to intervene and talk through the ideas they are forming. The language children use in the early stages of measuring or comparing objects such as 'big' can only be developed into 'long', 'heavy' or 'tall' by grasping every opportunity to model and rephrase their wording when working or playing alongside them. This will enable them to begin to understand how 'big' things can vary in length, weight or height rather than just seeing them as large objects.

Figure 2.1 Use familiar objects for promoting measuring, such as wellington boots, handprints and footprints.

Everyday experiences of measuring

- Bath time
- Cooking
- Shopping
- Meal times
- Creative activities such as cutting, sticking and making
- Getting dressed
- Bus and train timetables
- Television programme planners
- Clocks, watches and timers
- Appliances such as microwaves, ovens, telephones with digital displays and timer functions

What are the building blocks?

Length and distance

This is about children estimating, measuring, comparing and ordering lengths and distances. Children will begin by comparing using direct comparison and will then progress onto using uniform non-standard units such as cubes or straws. Once secure with non-standard units they will use standard units: metres and then centimetres, and will choose their own equipment for measuring.

Weight

This is about children estimating, weighing, comparing and ordering objects according to how heavy they are. Children will begin by comparing objects using direct comparison and will then progress onto using uniform non-standard units such as cubes. Once secure with non-standard units they will use standard units: kilograms and then grams, and will choose their own equipment for weighing.

Capacity

This is about children estimating, measuring, comparing and ordering containers according to how much they can hold. Children will begin by comparing capacities using direct comparison and will then progress onto using uniform non-standard units such as cubes or cups of rice. Once secure with non-standard units they will use standard units: litres and then millilitres, and will choose their own equipment for measuring.

Time

This is about children beginning to understand the passing of time within their own lives, from sequencing actions to complete a task to knowing the order that events occur during the day. Children will then learn how to measure time using sand timers and analogue clocks to tell the time to the hour and half hour. This learning is based on familiar experiences such as the time to wake up, go to bed, and have lunch. It is also important for them to understand how this measurement of time builds into days, weeks, months and seasons of the year.

Comparison

This is about children making comparisons between objects and measurements to make sense of the world around them. Comparison is key within this area of mathematics as, before units of measurement are introduced, children can only establish if something is long, heavy or holds a lot if they have something to compare it to. It is the act of comparison that encourages language development within this area, building on from 'big' or 'long' to longer, longest, etc. They begin by comparing two objects or measurements through direct comparison, for example placing two objects next to each other to find out which is longer. They will then learn strategies to compare and order more than two and understand how measurements can support this comparison.

Conservation

This is about children using comparison to develop their mathematical thinking about things they encounter in their everyday lives. They will begin to explore how the same measurement does not always look the same, for example two containers that hold the same amount of water may be different shapes or sizes. Just as children struggle to understand that seven counters remain as seven no matter how they are arranged, they also are often under the illusion that big things weigh more or tall containers hold more. It is essential to provide experiences for children to discover the idea of conservation through their play and talk through these concepts with children as they are working.

Accuracy

This is about children understanding that although they may make estimates when measuring, it is important that when using units of measurement they must work accurately. It is vital that children know why accuracy is important, for example inaccurate weighing when cooking could spoil the taste of a cake. Demonstrating how to use measuring equipment correctly and accurately, even when children are very young, is therefore essential.

Key vocabulary

- Length
- Capacity
- Weight
- Distance
- Time
- Near/nearest/far/further/furthest
- Heavy/heavier/heaviest
- Light/lighter/lightest
- Kilogram
- Gram
- Balances
- Scales
- Full
- Empty
- Half full/empty
- Nearly full/empty
- Holds most/least
- Container
- Litre
- Millilitre
- Short/shorter/shortest
- Long/longer/longest
- Metre
- Centimetre
- Order
- Measure
- Estimate
- Accurate
- Unit of measurement

Moving on:
What does it look like at the three stages of progression?

Laying the foundations
Children at this stage:

- begin to categorise objects according to properties, for example size;
- begin to use the language of size;
- understand some talk about the immediate past or future, such as 'before', 'later', 'soon';
- anticipate familiar time-based events such as meal times.

Beginning to build
Children at this stage:

- compare quantities using words such as 'heavier', 'lighter';
- order two, then three items by weight, height, capacity and length;
- order and sequence familiar events;
- use everyday language relating to time;
- begin to measure short periods of time.

Building up
Children at this stage:

- compare, describe and solve practical problems for height, lengths, mass, weight, capacity and time;
- measure and begin to record the following: lengths and heights, mass, weight, capacity and time, choosing and using uniform and non-standard or standard units and measuring equipment;
- order events using time related language such as before and after, next, first, today, yesterday, tomorrow, morning, afternoon and evening;
- use language relating to days of the week, months and years;
- tell the time to the hour and half past the hour and represent these on a clock face.

Building together

Sleepy animals
Building blocks:

- Length
- Accuracy

Moving on:

Laying the foundations

You will need:

Sticks of varying lengths, twigs, leaves, soft toy creatures, clipboards, pencils, paper, cubes, straws

Main activity:

Hide some soft toy creatures in trees or bushes in the outdoor area. Explain that these creatures need somewhere to sleep and that the children will be creating beds for them using natural resources. Provide the children with a range of sticks of varying lengths, leaves and twigs. Look at the resources and compare the sticks that have been collected. Can the children find the longest stick? Can they find the shortest stick? Encourage the children to talk about the sticks as they look at them and model mathematical language as they talk. Children then find a soft toy and choose resources to build a flat bed for it. Talk to the children about their choices, such as the length of the sticks: why did they choose those? Have they chosen long or short sticks? As the children are making the bed talk to them about what they are doing and pose questions, such as 'Are the sides of your bed long enough for your creature?', 'Do you need more sticks to make your bed longer?' Once the children have made their bed ask them to check that their creature fits inside. If it is not big enough discuss how to make it bigger and model the language of 'longer' when describing the sides of the bed. What if they had a bigger or smaller creature, could they change their bed to make it the correct size?

Make it easier: Instead of children building their own beds have some that have already been made using sticks. Children can then match the creatures to the beds that they fit inside. Talk to the children about how they decide which creature could sleep in which bed. As they test their ideas model language to describe what they can see, such as 'That bed is too small'.

Make it harder: Use the main activity but also provide some non-standard units, such as cubes or straws. Can the children measure how long the bed is that they have made for their creature? Who has made the longest bed? Who has made the shortest bed? Provide additional challenges, such as 'Can you make a bed that is 20 cubes long?' Give children clipboards and paper to allow them to record what they have done using pictures, marks and numerals.

Out and about

Treasure maps
Building blocks:

- Distance
- Conservation
- Accuracy

Moving on:

Beginning to build

You will need:

Clipboards, paper, pens/pencils, straws, empty wrapping paper rolls, sticks that are all of equal length, shiny objects, plastic/real coins, metre sticks, trundle wheels

Main activity:

Tell the children that they are going to pretend to be pirates. They have stolen some treasure and need to bury it, but so that they do not forget its location they will need to make treasure maps. Choose an area of the outdoor environment for children to bury their treasure (shiny objects, plastic or real coins). Now either look for or set up some landmarks that children will use on their maps, such as trees, rocks, flower beds, a pile of logs, a tower of boxes (mountain), etc. Talk to the children about how to create instructions using these landmarks as points to measure from: how far is the treasure from the tall oak tree? How will they measure the distance between two points? Discuss their ideas and highlight the importance of ensuring that the unit of measurement they are using is uniform: that each unit is the same size. For example, using their feet to measure by placing them toe-to-toe but not leaving gaps between their shoes, or using sticks that are all the same length and ensuring the sticks are touching with no gaps or overlaps. Support children in measuring the distance from the treasure to a landmark. Children then record this distance on the map by drawing the treasure and the landmark and choose a way to show the measurements they have completed. Model using a range of uniform non-standard units, such as sticks and cardboard rolls/tubes, to measure the distance. How many do they need to span the distance between the treasure and the landmark? Compare how many of each non-standard unit you needed; which did you need the most/least of? Highlight that although you have used different units the distance remains the same, so, for example eight sticks were needed compared to only five cardboard tubes. Place the units next to each other in lines to show that they measure the same distance and are the same length overall. Now challenge children to find a second landmark and to measure the distance from their first landmark to it. Compare children's work; what non-standard unit did they choose to use? How did they measure the distance? Did they measure it accurately? How have they recorded what they have done?

Make it easier: Use the same activity but instead of measuring the distance between the two points talk to the children about how they would describe where the treasure is compared to other landmarks using everyday language. For example they could state 'the treasure is near the tree' or 'it is far away from the path'. They could then attempt the treasure hunt with friends using these and other simple instructions, such as 'closer', when children are trying to find their treasure and are moving around the outdoor environment.

Make it harder: Use the same activity but instead of using non-standard units introduce the concept of one metre to measure the distance between two points. Model how to use a metre stick or trundle wheel to measure the distance to the nearest metre. Demonstrate how to record the measurements using the number followed by 'm'.

Out and about

Throwing challenge

Building blocks:

- Length
- Distance
- Comparison
- Accuracy

Moving on:

Building up

You will need:

Beanbags, metre sticks, tape measures, strips of paper, cubes, rulers, clipboards, pens/pencils, shoes/wellies, paint, paper

Main activity:

Explain that the children have a challenge to solve: 'Do children with bigger hands throw further?' How could they solve this problem? What do they need to find out? Share ideas and talk about the information they will need to collect: measurements of children's hands and measurements of how far they can throw. Ask children to make predictions about whether they think the answer to the question will be 'yes' or 'no', and the reasoning behind their thinking. What is the best way to measure how big a hand is? Talk about measuring the width/length of the hand span. Discuss the units they could use and equipment they might need. Follow children's ideas and allow time for them to investigate how to measure each other's hand spans. Prompt the use of non-standard units such as cubes for measuring. How could the children record what they have found out? Use a simple table to record the findings with a list of hand spans from the longest to the shortest. Repeat this process now focusing on finding out how far each child can throw. Talk about how this involves measuring the distance the beanbag travels. When discussing suitable units of measurement and equipment, introduce the use of a metre stick, if it is not suggested. Throws could be described as 'longer than three metres' or 'just shorter than two metres'. Record results in a table and then use this and the table of hand spans to draw conclusions and to answer the question 'Do children with bigger hands throw further?' Were their predictions right? Did their findings surprise them?

Make it easier: Repeat the same structure but alter the investigation to 'Who would make the longest footprint?' Children should suggest and try out ideas to answer the question using shoes or wellies to make footprints by printing using paint. They can then decide how to measure which is the longest. Methods children could attempt could include direct comparison of two footprints to see which is longer or shorter, or using uniform non-standard units such as cubes to measure the footprint. Results could be recorded by an adult using a simple table and children could talk about who had the longest and shortest print.

Make it harder: Repeat the same investigation but prompt children to use rulers instead of non-standard units to measure hand spans to the nearest centimetre. When they are measuring the distance the beanbag has travelled encourage them to read the marked intervals on the metre stick to measure in metres and centimetres rather than just to the nearest metre.

Puzzles and games

Sands of time
Building blocks:

- Time
- Conservation

Moving on:

Laying the foundations

You will need:

Sand timers of varying durations, building bricks, clipboards, pencils/pens, funnels, cups with holes, sand

Main activity:

Leave sand timers in areas where children play, to allow them to explore how they work before showing them their function. Talk to the children about what they think the sand timer could be used for. Show the children what happens if the sand timer is turned over. Count aloud whilst the sand drains through, encouraging the children to join in. Set up small activity stations with the children of things they could practise within the time it takes for the sand to run out. Pose questions to challenge the children such as 'How many times can you jump before the sand timer runs out?' or 'How many bricks can you put together in a tower?' Help the children to count the number of times they complete each activity and provide clipboards with a range of writing tools to encourage them to record their results in their own way. Children could be given the opportunity to make their own simple sand timers, for example, using a funnel (with its pipe covered) attached to the top of a container so that the sand flows once the pipe is uncovered, or by using cups with small holes in that provide a slow flow of sand once lifted up. Which of their sand timers runs out quickly/slowly?

Make it easier: Whilst children are playing, for example pouring and filling in the sand tray, building with construction equipment or dressing up, use the simple language of time such as 'before', 'after' and 'soon' to talk about what they are doing, such as 'after dressing up you can work at the sand tray'.

Make it harder: Use sand timers of different time durations and compare the number of things they could do in one, two or five minutes. Talk about activities they do in their everyday life that could be done in the time it takes for the sand to run out, for example is it long enough to have a bath? Eat their lunch? Put their coat on? Discuss their understanding of longer lengths of time and how time is used to order/sequence events in our daily lives.

Puzzles and games

Jigsaws
Building blocks:

* Time

Moving on:

Beginning to build

You will need:

Card with pictures of familiar events drawn on made into jigsaw pieces, blank card jigsaw pieces, folded paper for diaries

Main activity:

Make a simple picture comic strip of activities that children complete throughout the day such as waking up, getting dressed, eating lunch, having a bath and going to sleep. Cut the comic strip of pictures into shaped pieces to make a jigsaw. Show children the pictures in the incorrect order. Can they reorganise them into the correct order to complete the jigsaw? Talk through the activities they complete and why they are in that order. What would happen if they went to sleep before having a bath? Do the children know times of any of these activities in their days? Talk about their routines, are there any other things that they do every day? Where would these come in the order of the jigsaw pictures? Working with a small group of children, talk about a familiar task such as brushing teeth. Ask the children to talk through the steps in order and then draw pictures of each step on blank jigsaw pieces. Can they then order the pictures to complete the jigsaw? Talk about their choices and why they have put their pictures in that order. What would happen if they put toothpaste on the brush after brushing their teeth? What other activities can they think of to order? Challenge children to make an independent jigsaw based on another familiar task, such as building a snowman, getting dressed, making a sandwich, etc. They can then give their jigsaw to another child to complete and talk together about the order of events.

Make it easier: Create a visual timetable with a small number of pictures, such as three, with key events that happen during the day such as snack time, going home, eating lunch, etc. Talk to the children about the timetable, using simple language, such as 'later we will have lunch' or 'it is time to go home soon'. Remove pictures as events are completed and encourage children to look at the timetable throughout the day to remind them of what will happen next.

Make it harder: Include o'clock times on pictures of familiar events such as wake up at seven o'clock, start school at nine o'clock, eat lunch at twelve o'clock. Can the children use the o'clock times to order the pictures? Make simple diaries with the children showing tasks they complete in a day and ask children to draw o'clock times next to each activity to show when it is completed.

Puzzles and games

What's the time sleepyhead?

Building blocks:

- Time
- Accuracy

Moving on:

Building up

You will need:

Large and small individual geared analogue clocks, pictures of real life examples of analogue clocks

Main activity:

Talk about children's daily routines, such as getting up, getting dressed, arriving/ leaving school, having breakfast, lunch, dinner. What order do these events occur during a normal day? Do any of the children know at what times these events happen? What role do clocks play in our lives, especially when we are at school? Look at a large analogue clock with the hands set at nine o'clock. Can the children say what time it is? Identify the two different hands on the clock and discuss how each moves around it. What happens at nine o'clock on every weekday morning? Demonstrate how to make nine o'clock and other o'clock times using a geared clock. Allow children time to attempt o'clock times on individual clocks. Set up a game where an adult stands on one side of the room and children stand on the other. What time do most children wake up? Decide on an o'clock time to use in the following game. The adult pretends to be sleeping until the children shout 'What's the time sleepyhead?' The adult shows an o'clock time on a large clock. Children whisper the time that has been made so as not to wake the adult who goes back to 'sleep'. The children move one step closer every time they correctly identify the time on the clock. The game continues until the children reach the adult sleeping and shout 'wake up' or, the adult has shown the wake up time decided by the class, which ends the game and a child is then chosen to be the sleepyhead. The game can then be repeated by choosing different children to lead it. It can also be altered so that the sleepyhead whispers the time and every child has to make the time on their individual clock and those that make the time correctly take a step forwards.

Make it easier: Show children different images or a range of real analogue clocks. Look carefully at the position of the numbers on the clock face. Talk about why the numbers are in those positions and play some quick simple games where numbers are covered and children have to guess which numbers they cannot see. Play a different version of the sleepyhead game, the adult playing the role of sleepyhead calls out numbers from the clock face instead of times. Children have blank clock faces and they either place number cards or write the number that is called out in the correct place on the clock. If they place the number correctly they take one step towards sleepyhead.

Make it harder: Ask children if they know how to make 'half past' times. Demonstrate how to make half past times with the hour hand half way between the hour numbers and the minute hand on the number six. Play the sleepyhead game using half past times with children showing these times on individual clocks.

 ## *Cooking*

In the kitchen
Building blocks:

- Weight
- Comparison

Moving on:

Laying the foundations

You will need:

Cooking ingredients, e.g. flour, rice, pasta, lentils, couscous, pots, boxes or packets, bucket balances, scales, bags, shelves (or pictures of them)

Main activity:

Set up an area as a kitchen with a range of familiar cooking ingredients such as flour, rice, pasta, lentils and couscous all in pots. Explain that the children are going to be creating their own recipes for cooking by mixing ingredients together. Talk about what people at home use when they are cooking, such as useful utensils and appliances. How do we make sure we have the right amount of ingredients when we are cooking? Have a selection of scales that could be used to weigh ingredients and talk about how they work. Show children a bucket balance; how do they think they can use it to weigh ingredients in the kitchen? Demonstrate how to pour one ingredient in one bucket and talk about what happens. What then happens when you pour a different ingredient in the other bucket? Use the words 'heavy' and 'light' to describe what is happening to the buckets. Allow children time to explore the bucket balances by pouring and filling when working in the kitchen, watching what happens as they add or remove ingredients from the buckets. Talk to the children as they work, encouraging them to describe what is happening to the buckets. Pose questions such as 'What do you think would happen if we poured more flour in this bucket?' or 'What do you think would happen if we had less flour in this bucket?'

Make it easier: Within children's play or during everyday tasks talk to the children about how heavy or light objects are in comparison to others. For example, when carrying bags of shopping show children that because the bags are heavy they pull down on your arms and they are harder to lift. Set small challenges such as 'Which items in our kitchen cupboards are the hardest/easiest to lift?' Talk about their choices and how they can check if they were right. Encourage the use of words such as 'heavy' and 'light' and model this vocabulary whilst talking about what the children are doing.

Make it harder: Have packets and boxes of food in the pretend kitchen. Explain to the children that the heavy items need to go on the top shelf of the kitchen cupboard and the light items on the bottom shelf. How could they find out which items are heavy and which are light? Encourage them to hold an ingredient in each hand and feel how heavy they are compared to each other. Which would go on the top shelf and which would go on the bottom? Allow time for children to sort the items. How could they use a bucket balance to help them? Demonstrate how to compare two items using the bucket balance and discuss how you know which is heavier just by watching that bucket move downwards.

Cooking

All in a muddle

Building blocks:

- Weight
- Comparison

Moving on:

Beginning to build

You will need:

Two bags of sugar (one heavier, one lighter), two bags of flour (one heavier, one lighter), two packets of butter (one heavier, one lighter), balances, cubes, clipboards and paper

Main activity:

In a busy restaurant there are two chefs cooking two special cakes. One chef is in charge of cooking a small cake and the other chef is cooking a large cake. But they have got in a bit of a muddle with their ingredients and they do not know which ingredients belong to which chef. Show the children that there are two bags of sugar, two bags of flour and two packets of butter (pre-weighed and in sealed bags). The chefs know that the heavier items will be for the large cake and the lighter items for the small cake but they do not know how to find out which ingredients are the heavier/lighter ones. Can the children help? Talk through ideas that the children have to sort the ingredients into two sets. Allow children time holding the ingredients to make predictions about which are the heavier items for the large cake. Demonstrate how to use a bucket balance to find out which one is heavier/lighter using two objects. Talk about what they can see happening and encourage the use of the correct mathematical vocabulary. Provide pairs of children or individuals with bucket balances and a set of the muddled ingredients. Can they use the bucket balance to determine which ingredients are for the large cake? Observe the children and ask them to describe what is happening as they add or remove the ingredients. Compare their findings; do they all agree about which items are for each cake? Were their predictions right?

Make it easier: Make the difference between the heavier and lighter ingredients very obvious so that children can pick up the pairs of ingredients and order the two by direct comparison by holding them. Encourage them to hold their hands out in front of them and talk about how heavy each item feels using everyday language.

Make it harder: Introduce the concept of using uniform non-standard units such as cubes to find out how heavy each ingredient is. Put the ingredient in one side of the bucket balance and the cubes in the other. Talk about how to make the buckets balance. Can the children explain the choices they make to ensure both buckets weigh the same? Record how many cubes balance each ingredient and then compare to find the heavier/lighter of each pair.

Cooking

One kilogram

Building blocks:

- Weight
- Comparison
- Conservation
- Accuracy

Moving on:

Building up

You will need:

1kg bags/packets of flour and sugar, kilogram weights, cooking ingredients in packets, such as currants, butter, salt, baking soda, margarine, etc., bucket balances, non-standard units, such as cubes, straws, pennies, gram weights

Main activity:

Talk about how ingredients are packaged ready to sell in the shops. Looking at the packaging of 1kg bags of flour and sugar, can the children identify where it states on the packet how much sugar and flour there is in the packet? Discuss children's ideas and if necessary point out where it states 1kg on each packet. Do the children know what 1kg means? Talk about their ideas and show them a 1kg weight. Explain that there is a standard measure called the kilogram to show how heavy something is, which is especially useful if the contents cannot be counted, as in the case of sugar. Allow the children to hold the packets of flour and sugar and the 1kg weight to get an idea about how heavy a kilogram is. Show the children a bag of new cooking ingredients such as a large bag of currants (500g), a large bag of salt (1.5kg), baking soda/bicarbonate of soda (200g), a large tub of margarine (1kg). Challenge the children to sort the ingredients into three groups; those that weigh 1kg, those that are heavier than 1kg and those that are lighter than 1kg. Let the children hold the ingredients and make estimates and sort them, talking about the reasons for their choices. How can they check if they are right? Listen to suggestions and prompt the use of a bucket balance if it is not suggested. Demonstrate how to check one ingredient by putting the 1kg weight in one bucket and the ingredient in the other. What does it mean if the bucket moves up/down/remains balanced? Let children check the other ingredients using the 1kg and the bucket balance. Were any of their guesses correct?

Make it easier: Talk to the children about how to weigh ingredients for cooking. Show the children some small bags of ingredients such as flour, sugar, raisins and marshmallows that have been weighed using non-standard units that the children will use, such as cubes. Talk to them about how they think they could use the bucket balance to find out how heavy the ingredients are. Try some of their ideas and prompt them to think about what they could use to determine how heavy each ingredient is compared to the others. Discuss non-standard units and the fact that they have to be identical units: the same size and shape such as cubes, straws, pennies, etc. demonstrate how to weigh the ingredients using cubes in the bucket balance. Provide the children with a range of ingredients to weigh and encourage them to record their findings. Discuss which was the heaviest/lightest ingredient and if any weighed the same.

Make it harder: Provide the children with a selection of gram weights and small bags of ingredients, as in 'Make it easier' but that have been weighed using grams in multiples of tens, such as 10g, 50g, 80g, etc. Talk about the gram weights, identifying the quantities and discussing which is heaviest and lightest. Can they find equivalent weights for a 50g weight? Explore using 10g and 20g weights to make a range of quantities before using them in the bucket balances. Allow children to use the bucket balances with gram weights to find out how much each item weighs. Ask children to record their findings using a simple table. Can they order three or five ingredients by weight using the results?

Water

Car wash
Building blocks:

- Capacity
- Comparison
- Accuracy
- Conservation

Moving on:

Building up

You will need:

Cars, bikes, scooters, large bowls, buckets, cups, watering cans, bottles, sponges, guttering, pipes, plastic tubes, spoons, large tray of water

Main activity:

Have a selection of cars/bikes/scooters that need to be washed and a range of different sized containers such as large bowls, buckets, cups, watering cans or bottles. Explain that the children will be setting up a car wash to clean all the dirty vehicles. Put large amounts of water in big buckets or trays and pose the question of how they will move the water to the car wash from the bucket/tray. Prompt them to use the containers that have been provided. Allow time for the children to enjoy filling the containers with water and then pouring it on the cars. Talk to them about what they are doing and encourage them to talk about the quantities of water needed to clean the vehicles, such as 'that is enough' or 'we will need more'. Model the language of capacity to describe how full their containers are as they fill them and discuss what happens to the quantity of water in their containers as they enjoy pouring and emptying the containers.

Make it easier: Provide a range of large equipment such as buckets, guttering, pipes, plastic tubes, cups, spoons, etc. and access to a source of water either from a tap or in a large tray. Work with children to fill containers and then enjoy pouring them through tubes, pipes and down the guttering. Talk about what is happening to the water as it is poured through different sized pipes, etc. Which containers are easiest to use to pour from? Which are harder? Why do they think this is?

Make it harder: Set a challenge for children to explore such as 'will it be quicker to wash the car using a bottle or cup?' What do they think the answer will be? Why? Observe the children as they use the equipment to explore the problem. Help the children to draw conclusions by talking them through what they have found out, for example, 'You only needed four bottles to wash the car but you needed fifteen cups so which do you think was quicker?' They can then think of their own problem involving two different containers to solve themselves or pose to other children.

Water

Party drinks
Building blocks:

- Capacity
- Comparison
- Conservation
- Accuracy

Moving on:

Beginning to build

You will need:

Small table with toys, cups, chairs, jugs of varying sizes, bowl or tray for holding water, egg cups, measuring spoons, clipboards, sticky notes, pens

Main activity:

Set up a small table for children or toys to be seated around for either a snack or pretend party. Start with only two chairs and a cup in front of each chair. Explain that there is room for two guests at the table and they each want a drink. Provide two or three different sized jugs full of water. Talk about how they could describe how much water is in the jugs, such as: 'they are full'. Which do they think would be the best size to provide enough water for two drinks? How could they find out? Test out some of the children's ideas and discuss whether each method helped you to find out more about the jugs. Suggest using each jug to fill the two cups, how much water is left in the jugs after filling the cups? What does that tell them about the jug? Encourage direct comparison between the jugs, talking about which holds more and less, and how they know this by looking at how much water is left in the jug. Establish which jug is best for filling two cups. Now set more places at the table, for example with five seats and again set the challenge of finding the best jug for the job. Is it the same jug as before? Did every jug have enough water in it to fill five cups? What does that tell us about the amount of water each jug can hold? After exploring, ask children which jug they think overall holds the most/least water. Talk about their ideas. Compare the capacities of the jugs by using one to fill another; is there enough/too much water to fill another jug? Use these discussions to make direct comparisons of the jugs' capacities.

Make it easier: Provide a range of cups and jugs in bowls or trays of water and allow time for children to explore pouring and filling. Talk to them as they do this about how much water they have in the jugs using vocabulary such as 'full', 'nearly full' and 'nearly empty'. Help them to make simple deductions about how much the jugs hold by comparing them as they pour and fill.

Make it harder: Provide a selection of five different sized jugs and containers such as cups, egg cups, measuring spoons, etc. Talk to the children about how they could find out which jug holds the most. Discuss their ideas and allow time to test these and talk about what they have found out. Introduce the notion of uniform non-standard units to measure capacity such as cups and how these can be used to compare capacities by finding out how many of the non-standard units it takes to fill each jug. Provide clipboards, sticky notes and pens for children to record their findings. Can the children order the jugs according to their capacities?

 ## Water

Bottle hunt
Building blocks:

- Capacity
- Comparison
- Conservation
- Accuracy

Moving on:

Building up

You will need:

Photos or pictures of the drinks aisle in a supermarket, a range of bottles and containers of different sizes and shapes, litre measuring jugs, cups, stickers

Main activity:

Show the children pictures of the drinks aisle from a local supermarket or online shopping website. Explain that the local supermarket has had a mix up with the bottles of drink as all the labels have been lost. In the drinks aisle bottles are grouped by how much they hold. There is a section of the aisle for bottles that hold one litre, a section for those holding more than one litre and a section for those holding less than one litre. Can the children help to find out which bottles belong in each section? How could they determine which containers hold one litre? Take suggestions from the children and provide time for them to test their ideas. The children should work in small groups. Give each group a one litre measuring jug, a selection of different sized and shaped bottles that hold less than, more than and exactly one litre. Ask them to discuss in their groups how to use the measuring jug to group the bottles by their capacities. Model successful strategies whilst the children are working.

Make it easier: Provide children with three empty bottles and ask them to find out which holds the most water. How can they solve this problem? Again, allow time for investigation. Prompt children to check using direct comparison, by pouring the contents of one bottle into another to see which holds the most. Extend this by using a non-standard unit of measure such as a cup. Demonstrate how this can be used to compare the capacities by finding out how many cups of water are used to fill each bottle.

Make it harder: Look carefully together at the measuring jug and discuss the marked intervals; what does each small line represent? Demonstrate how to measure quantities less than a litre using the jug. Can they now find out how much water each bottle in the group 'holds less than a litre' can hold? How are they using the marked intervals to help them? They can then record their findings on stickers and label the bottles. To extend them further ask the children to order the bottles according to their capacities. Discuss their findings and check their accuracy using the measuring jug.

Assessment and observation

- Do they talk about the comparisons they are making? What words do they use to describe these?
- How do they compare objects' length, weight or capacity?
- Do they work accurately?
- Can they order objects according to their length, weight or capacity?
- Can they talk about what they have found out?
- Can they use markings or recording to show what they have found out?

? Stumbling blocks

The child thinks that bigger objects are always heavier.

- Provide opportunities in different areas of provision for children to handle heavy objects that are small and light objects that are large.
- Use large sealed boxes filled with light objects such as feathers or cotton wool and small sealed boxes filled with heavy objects such as building bricks, sand or wooden beads. Ask children to guess which box they think will be heavier before lifting them. Allow them to then hold and feel boxes and talk about which are heavier and which are lighter. Were their guesses right? Talk about how it does not matter how big the box is, it depends on what it contains. Reveal the contents and encourage children to talk about what they have found out.
- Use packets and boxes of food from the supermarket to demonstrate small can be heavy. Use tins of golden syrup, small bags of sugar and large boxes of cereal and large bags of crisps. As before, children guess which are heavy and light before holding them. They then check their estimates and talk about whether the small or big packets/boxes are the heaviest.

The child thinks tall containers always hold more.

- Provide a range of different sized containers in the water tray to enable children to explore how much each container can hold when filling and pouring.
- Use different sized and shaped jugs in the snack area for drinks so that children experience that a smaller wider jug can hold as much water as a tall thin jug.
- Encourage children to make predictions when playing with water and containers about which can hold the most. Model how to check their predictions by pouring water from one container into another to see if will hold the same amount, more or less. Provide containers that are wide and shallow that hold more than tall, thin

containers. Did the children expect them to hold more? Talk about what they have found out.

- Use cups as a uniform non-standard unit to test which containers hold the most. Use a tall, thin cylinder and a wide, shallow dish (that holds more than the cylinder). Ask children to guess which container holds the most water. Children fill the cup and pour into the container until it is full. Which held the most? Was this what they expected?

The child does not use the correct starting point for objects when comparing or measuring length.

- Model how to compare two objects by direct comparison to find out which is longer using a piece of tape stuck to the floor or table as a starting point for where to place the end of both objects. Demonstrate that by laying them next to each other with their end touching the tape it allows them to find out which is longer and which is shorter. This can then be extended to comparing three objects and then ordering them on the tape from the longest to the shortest.
- Demonstrate how to use a tape measure or ruler to measure the length of an object by placing the end of the ruler/tape measure against the end of the object. Talk about what would happen if they did not line the object up with the end of the ruler; it would be inaccurate measuring.
- Provide a range of rulers and measuring tapes within areas of provision so that children can explore these in their play. Create a written or picture set of instructions for how to be successful at measuring with a ruler. Photos could be taken of children measuring accurately and displayed for others to use as a model to copy.

Useful tools

A range of different shaped and sized containers
Jugs, cups, spoons, measuring spoons, bottles, boxes
Litre jugs
Bucket balances
Kilogram weights
Scales
Clocks (analogue and digital)
Sand timers
Buckets
Water trays
Tape measures

Paper strips
Rulers
Metre sticks
Cubes

📖 Stories and rhymes

Stories

Who Sank the Boat? by Pamela Allen, 1988, Puffin.
The Bad-Tempered Ladybird by Eric Carle, 1977, Puffin.
Time to Get Out of the Bath, Shirley by John Burningham, 1994, Red Fox Picture Books.
Mr Wolf's Week by Colin Hawkins, 1995, Mammoth.
The Very Hungry Caterpillar by Eric Carle, 2002, Puffin.
Five Minutes' Peace by Jill Murphy, 2003, Walker.

Rhymes

'Hickory dickory dock'
'Rub a dub dub'
'Jack and Jill'
'The queen of hearts'
'Polly put the kettle on'

3 | Data handling

Introduction

Data handling can at times be overlooked in the maths curriculum. This said it is often an area that children and their teachers enjoy exploring together. Data handling can support and link wonderfully to other areas of learning such as finding out about the world by sorting bugs, supporting personal and social development by discussing personal preferences for TV programmes, or promoting healthy eating by considering favourite foods! Young children love maths that is personal to them and data handling offers endless opportunities for expressing likes and dislikes and an opportunity to explore and celebrate how everyone is different through looking at hair colour and eye colour. Certain more sensitive issues such as height, weight, shoe size or family size should be avoided as these could cause upset for children within the group. Data handling has three core elements for young children. The first is deciding on the question to be answered and collecting the data, the second is presenting the data and the third is analysing and interpreting the data. Obviously with very young children these will not all be relevant for every activity they do, but learning in this area sows the seeds for the data handling experiences they will encounter later in their education.

Figure 3.1 Self-registration activities such as those based around arrival at school/setting or snack times involve children in the data handling process as their very own information is sorted.

Everyday experiences of data handling

- Sorting and matching clothes and sets of objects, e.g. socks, gloves, plates and cups
- Packing shopping: cans, frozen, fruit, vegetables, meat
- Organising laundry: colours, whites, towels, bedding
- Sorting toys in play: cars by colour/type, farm animals, building bricks by size/colour/shape
- Self-registration: who is here each day?
- Matching games and puzzles
- Tidying up into pictorially labelled boxes or drawers
- Sorting books in a book box: stories, non-fiction, poetry
- Sorting children: girls, boys, hair colour, clothing

What are the building blocks?

Collecting

This is about children being involved in deciding what they want to find out and how they can collect the information. Children's interests and ideas are great starting points for this area.

Presenting

This is about children exploring ways of showing what they have found out. For the very youngest children this is about sorting and matching and identifying similarities and differences between groups of objects.

Interpreting

This is about children discussing and analysing the data they have collected, identifying what it shows, using language such as most, least, more, fewest and recognising similarities and differences between sets.

Key vocabulary

- Count
- Sort
- Group
- Set
- Match
- Same
- Different
- Most
- Least
- More
- Fewest
- Favourite
- Popular
- Common
- How many…
- Not.….

Moving on:
What does it look like at the three stages of progression?

Laying the foundations
Children at this stage:

- can compare sets and recognise whether they have the same amount or not;
- sort and match objects according to properties such as shape, size or colour;
- begin to record their maths in their own ways, using pictures and their own signs and symbols;
- talk about some ways in which they are similar and different to their friends and families.

Beginning to build
Children at this stage:

- look carefully and talk about similarities and differences, sorting to identify these;
- compare sets using language such as 'more' and 'fewer';
- record their maths in their own ways which they can explain and interpret using marks;
- find maths problems to solve in their own play that relate to their interests and ideas.

Building up
Children at this stage:

- answer questions by recording data in simple lists and tables;
- begin to present their data using practical resources such as pictures, objects or blocks to make sets or simple graphs, block graphs or pictograms;
- sort objects into groups using simple diagrams according to set criteria such as colour, shape, type and so on;
- can suggest their own criterion for sorting;
- begin to interpret data identifying most and least popular/common groups and comparing sets.

Building together

Out and about

Leaf match

Building blocks:

- Collecting
- Presenting
- Interpreting

Moving on:

Laying the foundations

You will need:

A range of leaves (collected before the session), sorting hoops, sticky back plastic

Main activity:

It is important not to begin with too many leaves as the children may find this confusing. Begin by presenting them with a few pairs of obviously different leaves, e.g. varying colour, shape and size. Put them out for the children to look at. Play some simple matching games. Hold one up, can they find one that looks the same? Encourage them to talk about what makes their leaf the same as the chosen one. 'Different' should also be introduced and children asked to find a leaf that looks different to the selected one, explaining why it is different. To develop language further instead of holding up a leaf, describe one giving clear clues. Can the children decide which leaf is being described? Hoops could be used to sort leaves into simple sets, initially with the criteria decided by an adult and recorded on simple pictorial labels, e.g. green leaves, red leaves or big leaves, little leaves. It is important even at this stage to introduce a large box around the edge of the sets, as any leaf which does not fit into one of the sets will need to go within this area... nothing can be left out! Children should be encouraged to think of their own sets and could make photographic, drawn or written labels to name the sets. It is worthwhile building up a set of leaves covered on both sides in sticky back plastic to use inside and outside for sorting, matching, threading, pattern and picture making and counting activities. Laminating leaves can end in disaster and should be avoided!

Make it easier: Spend time leaf hunting with children, talking about the shape, size and colour of leaves and finding matching ones together. Can the children find a leaf the same or different to one you show them?

Make it harder: Using the hoops, put a different leaf into each one and challenge the children to find some leaves in the setting garden, at home or perhaps at the park to bring back and add to the matching sets. Using masking tape or chalk, create a large box around the edge of the hoops for leaves that do not fit into either set. Explain to the children that, although they cannot fit into any of the hoops, they must go somewhere! Talk about why they have added their leaf to a particular set. What is the same about all the leaves in each set? What could the sets be called? The amounts within each set could be counted and the leaves could be put into lines to make a simple graph, ensuring that all leaves are equally spaced. A simple squared grid could be drawn on the ground with chalks or made with masking tape, with numbers going up the side for children to put leaves into lines and compare, which has most/least/same amount and differences between groups.

Out and about

Nature hunt
Building blocks:

- Collecting
- Presenting
- Interpreting

Moving on:

Beginning to build

You will need:

Small baskets or paper lunch bags with handles, interesting items to collect, e.g. shells, pebbles, cones, small toys and so on (hidden before the activity if necessary).

Main activity:

Challenge the children to investigate the outdoor area and fill their bags/baskets with ten interesting things. Explain that they can choose whatever they like as long as it is safe and allowed and that they can have more than one of each thing (reminders about berries, picking plants and touching litter will be needed!). Agree with the children an amount of time they will have to complete this task, and use a timer to measure this. Set the children off to collect their items. If your area is lacking in natural resources, you could add some around the garden, such as shells, pebbles, cones, or even small toys, or pictures pegged up/hidden around the area. Once the children have collected their objects, bring them back together and empty the bags. Compare what different children have collected, e.g. 'You have more pebbles than your friend.' or 'You have got the same number of shells.' Talk to the children about how we could sort all the things they found either individually or as a whole group. You could model putting things into sets in hoops, or putting them into rows to make a simple graph. Listen to the ideas the children have primarily and make sure you try their ideas first. Talk together about what the data shows. Ask the children to tell you something about what they can see such as 'I have more shells than pebbles.' or 'We have the most cones.' The children could come up with ways of how their sorting could be put on the wall to make a display before it all blows away, for example by taking photos or drawing pictures.

Make it easier: Provide a collection of objects for the children to sort into hoops such as cones, pebbles, shells, leaves. Help children to decide which hoop will contain pebbles and label this using a pebble. Then decide which will contain cones and label this with a cone. Repeat this for the other objects. Challenge the children to sort the remaining objects into the correct hoops.

Make it harder: Children could collect up to 20 items in their bags and use these individually to make their own data set (more objects and pictures may need to be hidden for this to be viable). Once children have sorted what they found provide them with squares of paper to transfer their data to so that on each square they draw one of the collected items. Challenge them to use these pictures to present their data. Children could then progress to choosing a colour for each set of objects and use coloured bricks or cubes to make their own block graphs. Encourage children to not only tell you something about their data, but encourage them to also pose questions about their own data set for others to answer: 'How many shells did I collect?', 'How many more pebbles did I find than cones?'

Out and about

Information detectives!

Building blocks:

- Collecting
- Presenting
- Interpreting

Moving on:

Building up

You will need:

Mark making resources, e.g. whiteboards, pens, clipboards, paper, cameras and so on

Main activity:

This very open activity could be linked to a range of learning themes such as homes, minibeasts, trees, and traffic. Explain to the children that our world is full of information to find! Brainstorm with the children information that they could hunt for outside, begin by initially modelling some questions such as 'What is the most common door colour on the street outside?', 'Do more red or blue vehicles go past our school?' or 'Which type of tree is most common outside our school?' Encourage the children to share their ideas for questions they could answer outside, and then hold a vote to decide which one to investigate! Before collecting any information find out the children's ideas for how this could be done and value their contributions and agree some methods to use. Collect the information outside and return to the class to share this. Value the different ways children tried to record it, perhaps through pictures, tallies or drawings, and challenge them to think of ways they could present it to someone else, perhaps another child, teacher or headteacher. Provide hoops, squares of paper, sticky notes, number cards, cubes and counters, and work with children to choose resources to present their information, perhaps by making a block graph using cubes or pictures drawn in squares, or sorting pictures into hoops. Challenge them to explain what they have done and why they chose this way to present the data. What can they tell you about their information? Can they make up some questions about their data for a friend to answer?

Make it easier: Use play/real life situations to pose problems, perhaps by challenging children to help with sorting the beanbags or balls in the shed to find out which colour there is most of or perhaps, after hiding some coloured pieces of wool in the garden in three or four colours (these are worms or caterpillars), ask questions such as 'Are there more red or blue worms/caterpillars in the garden?' Whatever the question is, ask the children how they could find out and record their ideas. What will they need to take with them to find out? Encourage the children to go outside to find the answer to the question, then work together to look at what they found out.

Make it harder: The main activity outlined above could be simply differentiated to match the needs of children operating at a more advanced level, by introducing other ways to present and organise data such as tally charts, simple tables and lists. The concept of 'not' needs to be explored with children as they interpret their data: 'How many cars that go past our school are not red?', 'How many trees are not oak trees?'

 ## *Puzzles and games*

Welly match
Building blocks:

- Collecting
- Presenting
- Interpreting

Moving on:

Laying the foundations

You will need:

Children's wellingtons and pegs

Main activity:

Before the children begin the activity, prepare by mixing up the children's wellies in a messy pile (make sure they are named inside before though!) Tell the children that the wellies have been muddled up. If you are currently enjoying a story with them with a main character perhaps they could have been responsible and have sent a letter apologising, explaining they were looking for their own wellies. Ask the children if they have any ideas about how this mess could be tidied up and value these. Work with the children to sort the wellies and provide clothes pegs so that pairs can be pegged together. Put some pairs together incorrectly on purpose and observe the children's response to this. Talk about how the incorrect pair are the same and different, for example they are both red, but one has fire engines on it and so on. Once the wellies are all in pairs, talk about how they could be lined up to look tidy, perhaps putting them in rows according to colour, design and so on. Where wellies are almost the same (e.g. the same design but different sizes, heights, colours) ask the children to think of some reasons why they should go together and why they should not!

Make it easier: Use fewer pairs of wellies that are clearly very different, for example just using plain colours to make it easier for children to match.

Make it harder: Sort single wellies into hoops and as the problem naturally arises explore what happens when a welly fits into both hoops, e.g. pink and spotty (i.e. the wellies go in the intersecting section of both hoops). Remember to have the box around the edge of the wellies, for any wellies that do not fit into the hoops. Alternatively, the wellies could be put into rows to make simple graphs with numbers going along the side. Children could decide their own criteria for each row, e.g. blue wellies, pink wellies and so on. Encourage children to tell you something about what the information shows and ask and answer simple questions about it.

Puzzles and games

Roll it!

Building blocks:

- Collecting
- Presenting
- Interpreting

Moving on:

Beginning to build

You will need:

Mark making materials, e.g. whiteboards, clipboards, pens, one-to-six spotted dice, a prepared key to put on the wall and prepared outlines (see main activity)

Main activity:

This activity can be linked to many themes, topics and favourite stories. The activity is based on rolling a dice and following instructions to complete a picture. For example, if enjoying a story about underwear, provide an outline for each child of a pair of pants. Prepare a key to show what the rolled dice represents e.g. one for a spot, two for a stripe, three for a wavy line, four for a heart, five for a square, six for a '?' (you choose). Children play either individually or as a group and each time as the dice is rolled they refer to the key and draw the corresponding pattern on to their outline (the number is telling them what to draw, not how many. It is best just to draw one of whatever is rolled at a time initially, for example if a two was rolled, this means add a stripe). This is a very versatile activity and could be linked to aliens or monsters (where children add body parts), clothing (children add patterns), imaginary vehicles (children add big wheels, small wheels, doors, windows and exhaust pipes), footballs or balloons (where they add patterns/shapes), houses (where they add features) and so on. It is vital there is always a '?' as this enables children to make their own choices. Where children are rolling the dice individually within the group there are lots of opportunities after a few rolls each to compare pictures with someone else and ask questions such as 'What is the same/different?' or 'Tell me something about your pants/vehicle/alien' and so on. As children get more confident they can help to think of the keys before play starts. Once their picture is completed they could make a list of how many of each item is on their picture to find out which number was rolled most/least during the game.

Make it easier: Prepare a large dice for the group to use, perhaps on a large cube shaped box (such as a tissue box) or by using one of the commercially produced dice with slots to fit pictures into. Put the six pictures being used for the activity onto the dice directly instead of using a numbered dice and a key. Children roll the dice and add the rolled picture/pattern or feature to their picture. This could also be played as a group with one large outline that children add to instead of completing individual pictures.

Make it harder: Add a spotted dice to the game. Children now roll two dice. Use one dice with the features stuck to each side and a spotted dice to tell them how many to draw of the feature. After a few rolls, the children could use their picture to complete a simple table or chart showing how many of each thing they have drawn to find out what they have most/least of. Encourage them to make up some questions for a friend to answer about their picture.

Puzzles and games

Gate keeper

Building blocks:

- Collecting
- Presenting
- Interpreting

Moving on:

Building up

You will need:

Two hoops, two labels (one saying 'yes', one saying 'no'), objects or pictures to sort related to the theme (see main activity), props to turn the adult into the main character of the game (see main activity)

Main activity:

This activity works well with large groups. It is versatile and can be related to many themes, topics and favourite stories. It is based around the idea of a key character letting some items into sets and turning some away, leaving the children to look at the data and consider what the criteria could be for being allowed in. This activity can easily be linked to many favourite stories, perhaps an alien is only letting certain underwear into the space ship to take home, or a baker will only allow certain gingerbread people into the oven, maybe a fussy child will only accept certain birthday presents, the possibilities are limitless. The most important thing is to have prepared clear variable pictures of the items to be sorted and to decide on the criteria of who/what will be accepted before the game starts. If sorting underpants the variables could be spotted, striped, various colours or if using gingerbread people they could be happy, sad, with hats, without hats, varying numbers of buttons and so on. There need to be enough criteria to form sets. Each child is given a picture card and the adult in the key role of the character explains their dilemma (that they will only be letting certain types in, or they only like certain things, whilst not revealing the criteria). Show the children the 'yes' and 'no' sets and explain that some things will be allowed and some will not. The challenge is for the children to watch the 'yes' and 'no' sets growing and try to work out what the adult's rule is, for example 'only spotted pants' or 'only happy gingerbread people'. Each child approaches the adult presenting their picture and the adult looks carefully at it before telling the child whether or not it is allowed in the oven/space ship or whatever the context is. The child then puts it into the 'yes' or 'no' set. As the children approach and the sets begin to grow encourage them to make predictions about what the criteria could be. Once everyone has had a turn, reveal the criteria and encourage children to take on the lead role.

Make it easier: Provide simple pictures which involve sorting by type, for example, if using toys, provide different types of toys instead of variations as outlined above. Encourage the children to predict which ones will/will not be let in as the sets grow.

Make it harder: Differentiate the pictures provided and use two features in the criteria. Encourage the children to take on the key role and set their own criteria.

Favourite things

Snack time
Building blocks:

- Collecting
- Presenting
- Interpreting

Moving on:

Laying the foundations

You will need:

Clipboard and pens, children's names cards (with photos for younger children), snack area

Main activity:

Snack time is rich in opportunities to handle data. Whether children are selecting the correct photographs of fruit to match what is on offer each day for a 'menu' displayed on the wall, or sharing preferences about favourite foods, the mere fact that these activities are based around everyday meaningful contexts and also that they involve food makes snack time an opportunity for some real life maths! A simple clipboard left out at the snack table with a table featuring two columns, one with a happy face and one with a sad face, encourages children to record in their own ways (writing, drawing, making marks) whether or not they enjoyed the day's offerings. This can then be looked at together to find out whether most of the children enjoyed their snack.

Make it easier: Prepare photos of the children's faces and have these stuck on a wall near the snack area. Also display two large sheets of paper in different colours: one with a smiley face and 'Yum' in a speech bubble and one with a sad face and 'Yuk'. After the children have had their snack, they find their photo and stick it to either the 'yum' or 'yuk' set, providing information to discuss with the group.

Make it harder: Where children have a choice of snack, set up hoops or sheets of paper showing the different options as well as a 'no snack today' set. Once the children have chosen what they would like to have for their snack they add their name card or photo to the correct set. This could be adapted into building a simple block graph, where children's names or photos are in squares and a simple axis is set up on the wall with options along the bottom and numbers up the side. Children could then attach their photos to build the graph. This approach could also be taken with the main activity where a graph could be built to show who liked/disliked the snack each day. If this was done each day as the snack changed and results recorded by an adult each day, by the end of the week there could be five data sets and questions could be asked about which were the most popular/unpopular snacks of the week.

Favourite things

Roll and collect

Building blocks:

- Collecting
- Presenting
- Interpreting

Moving on:

Beginning to build

You will need:

One-to-six numbered dice, a mixture of coloured sorting objects in five colours (e.g. coloured buttons, sorting toys, cotton reels, pegs and beads, a dice with sides reflecting the five colours plus one side with '?')

Main activity:

Roll and collect games are easily adaptable and not only support counting skills, but social skills too. Children take it in turns to roll both dice and collect what the dice tell them, e.g. five blue or three red objects. Having more than one type of object, e.g. not all rubber sorting toys, but buttons, pegs and cotton reels too, gives children more choices to make and adds interest to the activity. When a '?' is rolled, children can choose which colour objects to select! Once everyone has had a few rolls each and has built up a good assortment of objects, challenge the children to sort their items to show you what they have collected. Children could sort into coloured sets, or sort by type, e.g. pegs, cotton reels, animals and so on. What can they tell you about their set? Can they ask a friend a question about the set such as 'How many red things do I have?', 'Which colour do I have most/least of?' and so on. Provide sticky notes for the children to make labels for their sets. Provide some mark making materials such as clipboards and paper. How can they record their sets so that they do not forget them at tidy up time?

Make it easier: Use just one type of object, e.g. threading buttons or cotton reels and just use the colour dice. Each time the colour dice is rolled one object of that colour is collected. A simple 'one, one, two, two, three, three' dice could be introduced once the children become familiar with the activity.

Make it harder: Play the game as set out in the main activity above, but also provide some coloured interconnecting cubes in the five colours. Once the children have finished rolling and collecting, challenge them to collect the correct cubes to match their sets and build this into a block graph. This could then be transferred to large squared paper, with squares coloured in the matching colours and numbers up the side.

Favourite things

Present time

Building blocks:

- Collecting
- Presenting
- Interpreting

Moving on:

Building up

You will need:

Toy catalogues, party bags, scissors

Main activity:

Give each child a party bag (ideally a paper bag with handles they can decorate themselves) with a pictorial label on the back such as dolls, vehicles, soft toys, computer games, action figures, garden toys and so on. Challenge the children to hunt through the catalogues for up to ten toys that could go into their bags. Can they find ten things, then cut them out and put them into their bags? Once they have done this, remove the label from the back of the bag and show the contents of the bag to some other children. If they look at what is inside the bag, what label do they think should go on to it? Talk about what is the same and different about the toys in the bag. The bags could also be used for sorting games, as children empty the bags, mix the pictures and sort them back into the bags matching the labels on them. Can they think of other labels to put on the bags instead of just sorting by type, e.g. sorting by material? Colour? Size?

Make it easier: Use real toys for sorting into hoops, with clearly prepared labels showing the sets.

Make it harder: Play a deduction type game by cutting out a selection of pictures of toys, perhaps 10 or 20, including some that are similar and different. Laminate these and colour photocopy them to make an identical board. Each child in a pair chooses a present from the board and keeps this secret. The children ask each other 'yes' or 'no' questions to try and work out which toy has been chosen, crossing out those that are eliminated with a dry wipe marker. Keep a tally of how many questions they need to ask before they find the answer!

All about me

Self-registration
Building blocks:

- Collecting
- Presenting
- Interpreting

Moving on:

Beginning to build

You will need:

Photos of the children laminated or name cards, question cards, 'yes' and 'no' labels/sheets

Main activity:

Self-registration is full of data handling potential and some simple additions to the routine can promote sorting, matching and comparing. Prepare some 'yes' and 'no' sets either in hoops or on paper, again with the box around the outside for anyone who does not fit into either set. Build up some photos to reflect children's favourite activities, sports, films, foods, television programmes and laminate these. Prepare a 'Do you like...' sign and each day display this with one of the pictures attached to form a question for children to answer as they enter the setting such as 'Do you like football?' or 'Do you like baked beans?' Children, on arrival at the setting, read the question and put their name card/photo into the 'yes' or 'no' set. Once everyone is present, the discussion can be had about where to put anyone who is absent as they are not able to answer the question (a great way of modelling using the box around the sets for anyone who does not go into either group).

Make it easier: To simplify the activity children remove their photo from a set and attach it to a piece of paper titled 'I am here today'. Each day the photos in this set could be counted and compared to those children who are absent and still have photos on the wall.

Make it harder: Have a question such as 'Which is your favourite fruit/television program/film/food', etc. and provide five sheets with different options on, e.g. apple, banana, satsuma, pear, grapes. At the start of the day, children move their name card/photo onto the sheet that reflects their favourite. This could provide opportunities to compare sets and lead to work making graphs. Instead of moving photos, children could decide which pot (five pots labelled with photos of the options) to put a cube into. The cubes could then be made into towers to make a simple graph. Groups could be compared and questions asked about the data. Children could find ways to record this data so that it could be looked at on another day (i.e. once the cubes have been put away).

 All about me

People sort
Building blocks:

- Collecting
- Presenting
- Interpreting

Moving on:

Beginning to build

You will need:

children!

Main activity:

This game is great for outdoors in a large space with the whole group and is based around sorting people in different ways. Again it is crucial to carefully consider the criteria children will be sorted by and to make these impersonal such as colour of clothing, age, hair colour, eye colour or things they like instead of sensitive issues such as size or skin colour. Prepare some simple pictorial signs on A4 paper showing variations such as eye colour, hair colour, jumper colour, favourite TV characters, etc. Fix these around the room/space and challenge the children to put themselves with the right set. Once the children are in the groups, talk about what will happen now. Once they go inside the information will be lost. How could it be recorded? Photos? Lists? Tables? Model this with the group. Laminated photos of the children from head to toe could be cut out and used for sorting as a class after lots of experience of physically sorting themselves.

Make it easier: With the children sitting in a large circle, give simple instructions such as 'If you like strawberries stand up'. The children then change places with someone else who likes strawberries! Relate instructions to children's interests and preferences such as TV shows, games and activities to keep them interested.

Make it harder: Provide cubes and challenge children to use these to build towers to represent the sets, making a simple block graph. Again this could then be transferred to squared paper or coloured squares of paper could be arranged into towers, adding numbers at the side. Laminated thought or speech bubbles could be used for recording children's own ideas, comments and questions about the data sets such as: 'More people have brown hair than blonde' or 'Not very many children like watching…'.

All about me

Survey superstars!
Building blocks:

- Collecting
- Presenting
- Interpreting

Moving on:

Building up

You will need:

Clipboards, paper, pencils/pens, hoops and cubes

Main activity:

Model with the children how to carry out a simple survey. Do this on a large board and demonstrate how to make a simple chart with options down the side and a space next to each one. Model how to ask people about their preferences by asking a child 'Which do you like the best?' and giving them the options. Ask the children for their ideas about how to quickly and easily record this, e.g. making a mark, drawing a smiley face, etc. Value and try out the ideas they have, illustrating how it needs to be simple and quick to be effective. Ask some more children about their preferences and add these to the survey. Talk about what the survey is showing as more children's preferences are added, comparing groups. Invite the children to share their ideas about what they could ask friends about, e.g. favourite cars, films, sweets and so on, stress the fact that there should not be too many options and perhaps model this by reeling off a list of 20 options to a child to show how difficult this would be to manage! Children make up their own surveys and draw their own simple charts to record these using clipboards. Once they have completed their surveys talk about how they could present the data, e.g. making sets in hoops, making graphs using sticks of cubes and so on. Value the ideas they have for presenting their own data and allow them to try these out. Provide sticky notes for them to record their own comments about their data sets and to think of questions for others to answer about it.

Make it easier: Make a large survey on the board or a large piece of paper using pictures to illustrate the options. Children choose which fruit/TV show/activity, etc. is their favourite and add their photo onto the survey next to the correct picture. Talk about which is the most/least popular, count how many people are in each set and find the numerals to match. The photos of the children in each set could be arranged in lines to make it easier to see which was the most popular.

Make it harder: Introduce the ideas of using tally marks (four marks then the fifth through it) to make it easier to count how many are in each group. Provide squared paper for children to use to transfer their surveys into simple block graphs.

Assessment and observation

- Are children able to match objects?
- Can they sort and talk about how they have sorted?
- Do they identify similarities and differences between objects?
- Can they count how many are in a set and compare groups using language such as more/less/most/least/fewer/popular?
- Can they think of their own criteria for sorting?
- What ideas do they have for collecting, sorting and presenting their information?

Stumbling blocks

The stumbling blocks children are likely to encounter with regards to data handling are largely related to learning in other aspects of maths such as counting (e.g. difficulty accurately counting how many are in a set) and calculating (difficulty finding totals when adding groups together such as 'How many children like apples and oranges?'). Children who struggle to understand difference will find it difficult to work out questions such as 'How many more leaves are green than red?' Please refer to the calculating and counting chapters for ideas to overcome some of these more number-focused stumbling blocks.

The language of maths can also cause difficulties as children handle data. The 'useful vocabulary' list gives examples of some of the types of words practitioners need to model and promote when working with children, not just in guided teaching activities, but when playing, carrying out daily routines and when generally talking with children in everyday life.

Outlined below are some more specific stumbling blocks related to handling data.

When asked 'How many more than…' questions about data, the child says the number that is in the 'most' group as their answer.

- Reinforce 'How many more than…' by comparing sets to see how many extra one has than the other.

When using 'not' criteria, children continue to put data that 'is' into the set, e.g. putting green leaves into a set titled 'not green'.

- Use practical objects and physically remove the items that will not be allowed in the 'not' set. For example, if the criteria was 'not green' explain to the children that this means all the green ones are not allowed in and physically remove them.

- Use lots of 'not' criteria in everyday routines so children become familiar with the language:' Who is *not* having packed lunch today?'
- Make clear pictorial cards for sorting with a large cross going through a picture to symbolise 'not'.
- Develop a physical action for 'not', such as arms in a cross and use this with some practical sorting of children. For example, if you asked 'Who is not wearing a purple jumper?', the purple jumper children should put their arms in a cross and leave the set, leaving everyone else in the set!

Useful tools

Sorting hoops
Mark making materials, e.g. clipboards, large paper, squared paper, pencils, pens
Cotton reels
Buttons
Sorting toys
Clothes pegs
Wellingtons
Socks
Shoes
Gloves
Shells
Leaves
Fir cones
Outdoor space
Dice
Photos of the children to sort
Pictures of favourite television characters, films and programmes

Stories and rhymes

Stories

My Mum and Dad Make Me Laugh by Nick Sharratt, 2012, Walker.
The Queen's Knickers by Nicholas Allen, 2000, Red Fox.
Handa's Surprise by Eileen Browne, 2006, Walker.
Red Rockets and Rainbow Jelly by Nick Sharratt and Sue Heap, 2004, Puffin.
Socks by Nick Sharratt and Elizabeth Lindsay, 2013, David Fickling Books.

Rhymes

Develop simple chants with the children linked to preferences which they respond to by standing/sitting or getting into groups. For example, the adult could tap out on a drum 'Who likes apples?' and children who do like apples either stand or move into a group replying 'We like apples' in time to the drum. Once one group has formed (perhaps of those who like apples) repeat the chant, for example 'Who likes bananas?' and from the remaining children a new group forms, keep adding chants linked to them until everyone is in a group and use this to build graphs, sets and charts using the children themselves, cubes, tallies or squares of paper. This could be adapted to match the interests of the class and they could think of their own questions to chant to the group.

4 | Calculating

Introduction

Calculation is perhaps one of the areas of mathematics that learners can feel particularly challenged by or worried about, largely due to the fact that there is normally a right or wrong answer. Many of us may recall our own maths education and remember being taught 'to go next door and borrow one' when solving subtraction problems. This became a constantly repeated mantra for lots of learners, who had very little or no understanding of why going next door was needed, and how borrowing worked. Long division, addition and multiplication were also taught with their own set of instructions, giving learners the idea that as long as these instructions were followed the answer would be right, and it worked... but how many really knew why or could recognise when it had gone wrong from looking at an answer that was clearly incorrect? Thankfully maths education has progressed since these days and the focus is now on giving children a range of methods to solve calculation problems so that they can choose the most effective and appropriate one to use, depending on the problem that needs solving. Practitioners are almost like assistants in a DIY store, helping children to add tools to their mathematical tool box, so they know just which tool they need to use when a problem needs solving. For example if calculating $20 - 18$, would it be more efficient to take 18 away from 20, count back 18 from 20 or count on from 18 to 20? The very basis of calculation is number. Without firm foundations in number and counting, children will always struggle to be effective calculators. It is only when children develop and build a solid understanding of the pattern of numbers, where numbers are in relation to others and the connections between them that they will be able to work fluidly with them to add, subtract, divide and multiply.

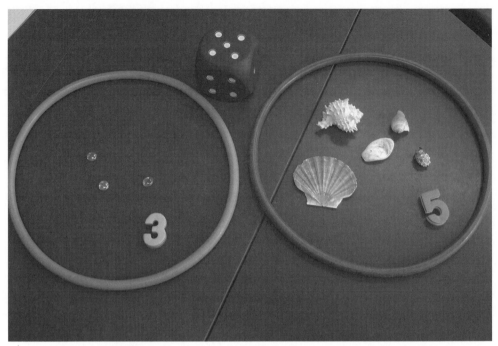

Figure 4.1 Young children need opportunities to develop a concrete understanding of more and less in order to grow into confident calculators.

Everyday experiences of calculating

- Snack time: is there enough…?
- Shopping
- Spending pocket money
- Buying penny sweets
- Working out scores in games/sports
- Cooking
- Setting the table
- Planning a party/picnic
- Registration/dinner registers

What are the building blocks?

Within calculation there are various important mathematical concepts and different core structures of the four operations. For the purpose of this practical book aimed at supporting the youngest children, the most relevant, developmentally appropriate concepts and structures are emphasised.

Addition

This is about children understanding two main structures of addition. The first one relates to 'altogether' where children understand that by putting two groups together there is a total, e.g. five dogs and three dogs would make eight dogs altogether. The second structure is related to counting on, for example if playing snakes and ladders, if a three is rolled whilst a player is on five, they count on three from five to reach eight. Although still recorded as $5 + 3 = 8$, this structure is not about combining two groups, but increasing a number. Children also need to learn that addition and multiplication are commutative (can be done in any order) i.e. $4 + 3 = 7$ and $3 + 4 = 7$. However, subtraction and division are not.

Subtraction

This is about young children understanding three main structures of subtraction. The first one children encounter in everyday life is 'taking away', for example you have five sweets and you eat two, how many are left?' The second structure is around 'difference', for example you have three sweets, and I have five, how many more do I have than you? This requires children to compare numbers to find how much more/fewer one has/is than the other. The third model is about counting back and is often demonstrated when working with number lines, tracks or board games. I am on five, I move back two and I am now on three. The taking away and counting back models clearly link to the altogether and counting on addition models respectively. In school/setting (and at home) there is a tendency to focus mainly on 'taking away'. Practitioners need to ensure that even the younger children have everyday relevant opportunities to explore the language of difference and counting back too!

Multiplying

This is about children understanding the most basic structure of multiplication, which is repeated addition, for example calculating that four lots of two is $2 + 2 + 2 + 2$ or 4×2.

Dividing

This is about children understanding the most basic structure of dividing, which is sharing into equal groups. For example there are six apples in the snack bowl and three children, how many will each one get?

Number patterns

This is about making connections between numbers and seeing patterns, for example counting in twos, fives and tens, or recognising odd and even numbers.

Recording calculations

This is about children being able to record calculations in their own ways. The emphasis in the early years must always be on developing a solid understanding of the practical aspect of calculation before children are expected to use symbols such as +, – and =, although as they progress in school and into Key Stage One it is important that they are familiar with what these signs mean and begin to use them when they are ready.

 # Key vocabulary

- Add, more, and, plus
- Make, sum, total
- Altogether
- Double
- One more, two more, ten more…
- Take (away), subtract
- One less, two less…, ten less…
- How many fewer is… than…?
- Difference between
- Is the same as
- Count on
- Count back
- +, −, =
- Lots of, groups of
- Share

Moving on:
What does it look like at the three stages of progression?

Laying the foundations
Children at this stage:

- show an interest in number problems during their play;
- recognise whether two groups of objects have the same number in or not;
- use everyday language to describe real life quantities (toys, snacks, etc.) such as more, most and a lot, not enough, not many;
- recognise that the amount within a group changes if some are added or removed;
- begin to record their maths in their own ways, using pictures and their own signs and symbols.

Beginning to build
Children at this stage:

- put two groups of objects together and count how many 'altogether', and can take some objects from a group, counting to find out how many are 'left';
- begin to use simple everyday vocabulary relating to addition and subtraction: altogether, add, take away, leaves, makes, more, less when engaged in practical activity;
- find their own problems to solve during play, e.g. in the role play area, small world area or at snack time;
- begin to add and subtract two single digit numbers using practical resources, e.g. toys, counting objects;
- begin to count on and back using number tracks (including games) and number lines;
- begin to develop an understanding of multiplication practically through counted repeated groups, e.g. pairs of socks or knives, fork and spoons at the table;
- begin to develop an understanding of division as sharing in practical contexts, e.g. snack time, tea parties, toys;
- may start to record their problems using some recognisable signs and symbols, e.g. numbers, +, – and =.

Building up
Children at this stage:

- count on and back to find an answer using number lines and are continuing to develop mental methods to do this;
- know that addition can be done in any order... but subtraction cannot!;
- record addition and subtraction problems using the +, – and = symbols;
- find the difference between two numbers by comparing quantities (e.g. towers of bricks) or counting up from one number to the other;
- begin to know some number facts by heart such as doubles and number bonds to ten and progressing to bonds within 20;
- count aloud in twos, fives, and tens;
- solve simple problems involving multiplication and division, by finding the answer using objects and pictures, progressing to arrays (with adult support);
- add and subtract one-digit and two-digit numbers to 20, including zero;
- solve simple word problems, showing their methods using signs, symbols, marks and pictures;
- solve simple problems that involve addition and subtraction, practically and using pictures.

Building together

Out and about

More or less
Building blocks:

- Addition
- Subtraction
- Recording

Moving on:

Laying the foundations

You will need:

Two large dice, one numbered or spotted one to six, the other with three smiley and three sad faces drawn/stuck on it, large numbers or chalks

Main activity:

This is a great outside activity for pairs of children or two small teams. Put the two hoops on the floor. Explain that each child will roll the dice and go and collect the matching number of objects (this could be anything from outside, twigs, pebbles, balls, etc.) and bring them back to their hoop as quickly as they can. When both players/teams have returned their items to their hoops, record the total in each hoop using the chalks or large numbers. Which one had the most? Which one had the least? Can the children show you the matching number of fingers for their hoops? You could find these numbers on a large outdoor number track or line and compare them. Then roll the smiley and sad face dice. If it lands on the smiley face, the 'most' team/player wins a point, if it lands on the sad face the 'least' team/player wins a point! The children can decide what to do if both hoops have the same number!

Make it easier: Use a 'one, one, two, two, three, three' dice and encourage children to roll and collect the number rolled and add to their set so they see the group getting bigger and bigger, using the language 'more' to reinforce this. Once they have ten objects perhaps they could roll again but remove objects from the set to see it becoming smaller.

Make it harder: Once both teams/players have collected their items, encourage them to find the difference between the two sets, perhaps by putting them into two parallel equally spaced lines to find how many more one has than the other, or find the numbers on a number line or track to compare and count on/back to find the difference.

Out and about

Tower fun!
Building blocks:

- Addition
- Subtraction
- Recording

Moving on:

Beginning to build

You will need:

Large building blocks either wooden or connecting plastic ones, two large dice, one with '+, +, +, –, –, –' and the other with 'one, one, two, two, three, three'

Main activity:

Another simple game for outside or in a large space. Children can work in pairs or teams to play. Ask them to begin by building a tower of six bricks. They then roll the +/– dice followed by the numbered dice to find out how many to add/subtract from their tower. Model the language of addition and subtraction as they add to and take from their towers. Can they work out how many there will be after they have added/removed bricks before they physically do it? Children can continue to play until their bricks have all gone, or their tower falls or is too tall to add to! Provide clipboards or whiteboards and ask them to find a way to draw what is happening to their tower. If children are playing against each other and building separate towers, these can be compared and the language of difference, more and fewer reinforced.

Make it easier: Begin with a tower of five bricks and use a large smiley and sad face dice, for children to roll. A smiley face means add one brick to the tower, a sad face means take one away. Reinforce the language of more and less/fewer as they build their tower. Can they predict how many will be in their tower before they add/remove one?

Make it harder: Children could record number sentences after each roll to show what has happened, e.g. a tower of five bricks has three added to it so... $5 + 3 = 8$. Talk about what happens if you roll more to subtract than you have? Remember not to tell children numbers cannot go below zero as they will learn as they progress through school that they can, instead explain that they cannot take away what they do not have and show this practically.

Out and about

Target practice

Building blocks:

- Addition
- Subtraction
- Number patterns
- Recording

Moving on:

Building up

You will need:

Beanbags, three different sized hoops, number cards, numerals or chalks, clipboards, whiteboards and pens, number lines or number squares

Main activity:

Set up the three hoops outside. Put/write the number two in the biggest hoop, five in the middle sized hoop and ten in the smallest hoop. Give each child five beanbags and challenge them to aim for the hoops. After they have thrown all the beanbags, challenge them to add their scores. Model adding the tens first, then fives and finally the twos to find the total. Encourage children to record this in their own ways. Any beanbags thrown outside of the hoops could result in points deducted from the total! Finding the total could then be shown on a number line or number square, adding tens, then fives, then twos before jumping back ones for missed targets.

Make it easier: Have the numbers one, two and three in the hoops. Children throw two bean bags then collect the matching number of small toys/pebbles/ shells, etc. from a bucket in each hoop. These could be counted altogether to find their total score. The numbers could be found on a number line or track to decide which number was bigger/smaller.

Make it harder: The score zones could be changed to numbers that are not so easy to add, e.g. three, four and six, however, ensure that resources are provided to support with finding these totals. Alternatively use two, five and ten and set scores for children to aim for, e.g. 30. They could be challenged to find all the combinations of beanbag throws that would give them a set total and record the related number sentences. The points deducted for beanbags missing the zones could be increased.

Puzzles and games

Welly jump!
Building blocks:

- Number pattern
- Recording

Moving on:

Laying the foundations

You will need:

Children's own wellington boots, a large roll of wallpaper, paint in trays, pens

Main activity:

This activity is better outside as it could get rather messy! Lay out the roll of paper and fix it to the floor with masking tape. Children put their wellies on and choose a colour paint to step into. They jump along the paper with their feet together and every time they land on the paper shout 'two' to signify two feet landing on the paper! These could then be cut out in pairs and put around the room to show repeated sets of two. You could put numbers with the welly prints to make a wellington boot print number track.

Make it easier: Let children explore making welly prints in pathways and practice counting these aloud together. Count how many jumps they can do!

Make it harder: Make welly prints, but as they jump practice counting in twos as their two feet land, count aloud 'two, four, six, eight, ten'. Cut out the pairs of welly prints when they are dried and number the wellies, either alternating two colours when writing the numbers or only writing the number on the second welly print of each pair so they record two, four, six, eight, ten.

Puzzles and games

The centipede's socks

Building blocks:

- Number patterns
- Recording

Moving on:

Beginning to build

You will need:

A washing line, clothes pegs, pairs of socks mixed in a pile, a large 'one, one, two, two, three, three' dice, an empty bucket/bowl (or with soapy water in, if working outside)

Main activity:

This activity would link well to a minibeast theme and could start with a letter from a giant centipede asking the children to wash his/her dirty socks. Start by explaining that the children will be rolling the dice to find out how many pairs of socks to wash each time. Make sure you remind the children it is pairs of socks, not individual socks, so, for example, a two rolled on the dice would mean two pairs of socks (four). The children then run to the pile of mixed up socks, find the correct number of matching pairs, wash them in the bucket and hang them on the washing line (clothes pegs are great for developing fine motor skills!). After each batch of washing, count the socks on the line in twos. When the washing line is full children could make pictures of the washing line recording the socks on it and matching numbers. Once the socks are dry they could roll the dice again to find out how many pairs to take down until the line is empty. Maybe they could make a giant centipede to wear all the socks.

Make it easier: Draw a large centipede/caterpillar with the children on a large roll of paper. Make sure the creature has lots of clearly defined legs. Children roll a 'one, one, two, two, three, three' dice and find the correct number of pairs of socks to put on his feet. Have the socks in pairs so the children go and collect the correct number of pairs, not individual socks! Maybe they could put some shoes or wellies on the creature too. Practice putting things into pairs such as boots, shoes, gloves and so on to reinforce the concept of 'pairs'.

Make it harder: Provide children with simple drawings of caterpillars/centipedes with up to 10 or 20 pairs of legs (i.e. 20 or 40 individual legs). As they roll their own individual one-to-six or 'one, one, two, two, three, three' dice they draw socks (or put on pre-cut sock shapes) on the correct number of legs, e.g. roll a three, draw three pairs of socks (i.e. six individual socks). The first person to put socks/shoes on all of their feet (agree a number before starting) is the winner! As they put the socks on their picture they could circle the numbers they are counting on a number square/number line (e.g. two, four, six, eight, etc.). Talk about the pattern. What do they notice? What would come next? Use these pictures to practice learning about counting in twos. Other number patterns could be explored through inventing aliens, monsters or imaginary animals with varying numbers of body parts: pairs of eyes for glasses, fingers for gloves and so on.

Puzzles and games

Body patterns
Building blocks:

- Number patterns
- Recording

Moving on:

Building up

You will need:

A large number square and dry wipe pen

Main activity:

Explain to the children that they will be making up some body patterns. Model this to start with. Ask one child to be in charge of the number square, putting circles around the numbers they hear you shouting. Start by focusing on the twos pattern. Model with the children how to clap low to one side and high to the other, whispering the number 'one' as you clap low, shouting 'two' as you clap high, whisper 'three' as you clap low, shout 'four' as you clap high and so on. The child with the number square circles only the shouted numbers, e.g. two, four, six, eight. Stop mid-clap and encourage children to predict the next numbers to be shouted by looking at the number square or thinking about the pattern so far. Count to at least 20, before stopping to look at the number square. What can the children tell you about the pattern? Work with the children to develop a body pattern for five. This could be left stamp (whisper 'one'), right stamp (whisper 'two'), left wave (whisper 'three'), right wave (whisper 'four'), head nod (shout 'five'), repeat only shouting loudly the head nod numbers (e.g. pattern of fives). Mark this on the number square in a different colour. What do the children notice? Which numbers are in the fives pattern? Are any in the twos pattern too? For a ten pattern children could use their fingers, only shouting the tens numbers aloud as they count the final finger or thumb. Children can develop their own patterns for counting. This is a great way to start a maths session!

Make it easier: Make up simple body patterns with the children, such as clap, stamp, clap, stamp, then extend these to include more than two movements. Count movements as you make them, not worrying about the whispering and shouting voices. Focus on the repeating pattern and counting aloud.

Make it harder: Challenge children to work in pairs to make up their own body patterns for other numbers, e.g. three, four, six, seven, and record the numbers they shout aloud. Encourage them to talk about the patterns they find and any numbers that come up in more than one pattern.

Shopping

Penny shop
Building blocks:

- Addition
- Subtraction
- Recording

Moving on:

Laying the foundations

You will need:

Pennies (real if possible), toys/objects to sell (could be related to your theme/children's interests), price tags, pens, shopping baskets, purses and wallets

Main activity:

Work with the children to set up a simple shop selling something they are interested in (toys, teddy bears, fruit, bags, hats or anything else they can think of). Label these with price tags initially up to 10p at the most. Take on the role of the shop keeper and invite children to come to your shop. Ideally another adult could take on the role of the shopper to model the sorts of language they would use in real life. Encourage the children to read the price tags for the item they want to purchase and count out the pennies from their purses or wallets to match the price tags to pay for the item. At this stage it would be useful to provide an image of the number on the tag such as spots in dice patterns for children still learning to recognise numerals.

Make it easier: Use lower prices up to 5p to support the children's basic counting skills if necessary. Focus on the idea of exchanging, i.e. you give the pennies and you get the item!

Make it harder: Ask the children to choose two items to purchase and work out the totals together. They could begin by getting the correct number of pennies for each item then count them altogether to find the total. Focus on ensuring they understand the value of a penny before introducing any other coins.

 Shopping

Party bag fun
Building blocks:

- Addition
- Subtraction
- Recording

Building up:

Beginning to build

You will need:

Party bags (either plastic commercial ones or paper takeaway handled paper bags the children have decorated themselves), pennies, small/interesting toys and objects (e.g. pebbles, marbles, shells, fir cones) to go into the party bags

Main activity:

This would link well to a birthday/celebration theme. The children could make and design their own party bags before the activity. Explain to the children that they will be buying special things to make party bags. Set up a small shop with lots of interesting small objects for them to choose from such as glass pebbles, shells, small toys and anything else that captures their imagination. Label these as various prices perhaps simple ones to start with, e.g. 1p, 2p, or 5p. Give the children a 5p to start and challenge them to spend all of their money buying items for their party bags. Compare how different children have filled their bags and model recording some of the related number sentences, not forgetting to introduce the 'p' as representing pence. You could stick the coins onto towers of interlocking cubes representing the correct amount using sticky tape to help the children understand that a 2p is worth two and a 5p is worth five. By having matching towers of cubes with the toys on sale, this would visually support them to understand what coins actually represent. This would also help children see that there is no 3p or 4p coin and that other coins must be used to make these totals. Model how to record the related number sentences when finding totals.

Make it easier: Make all items cost 1p. Label the dice with a picture of five items for sale plus a '?' for you to choose! Each child rolls the dice and has to pay a penny and take the shown item for their bag. A '?' means they can choose whichever item they like. Play until everyone has spent their 5p or 10p and then empty and compare the bags. How many pebbles did they buy? How many toys? Can they see anyone who bought more/fewer pebbles than them? This would lead into some great data handling work.

Make it harder: One child takes on the role of shopkeeper and has to give change to shoppers. Prices could be made trickier such as 6p or 8p, so that children are finding coins to make the amounts as there are no 6p and 8p coins. The total given to spend could be increased to 20p or more. When the contents of the bags are compared some simple pictograms could be made and purchases compared. When modelling how to give change, initially children could find this by taking away. Once they are confident with this, introduce using a finding the difference/ counting up model, for example if the total was 8p and the money given was a 10p coin, initially subtract eight from ten, either on a number line or using objects before progressing to counting up from eight to ten mentally or on a number line to work out the difference is 2p and this is the change needed. Children need to be very secure in counting to move to this and need to have had opportunities to start at and count onto and back from different numbers (such as start at seven, count to twelve), instead of just counting from one to ten or twenty repeatedly.

Shopping

Market day

Building blocks:

- Addition
- Subtraction
- Recording

Moving on:

Building up

You will need:

Tables, chairs, paper, pens, whiteboards, money, items to sell, purses, wallets and bags

Main activity:

This is a great whole class activity/project and can easily take up a day! Explain to the children that they will be setting up a whole class market. Look online for some clips of market places (please check the clip is appropriate before sharing it) as not all children may have been to a market before and watch these together to show what a hustling, bustling place a market is! Talk about how the stall holders encourage shoppers to come to them. Children can work in pairs or groups to decide what they want to sell at their stall and make price tags, posters and signs (e.g. persuasive posters and open and closed signs). Arrange the furniture in the room so tables are around the edge of the room and let children set up their stalls. Half the class take on the role of shoppers, visiting stalls and spending money. The sellers work out totals, give change and so on. The shoppers just decide where to spend their money. Work with the stall holders as they work out simple totals and model counting up to give change, either mentally or using a number line. Perhaps you could announce a sale where all prices are reduced by 1p/2p/10p or more. Can stall holders change their price labels to reflect this? Talk to the shoppers about how they are going to spend their money… will they buy lots of little items or perhaps just one or two large ones? Children could then swap roles so they experience buying and selling. This sort of role play activity will offer endless opportunities to solve real, relevant problems and encourage use of mathematical vocabulary.

Make it easier: Set up some stalls with items costing amounts to 5p or 10p. Give the shoppers pennies to buy with. Take on the role of the shop keeper to model the sort of language used and methods to find totals.

Make it harder: Increase prices to include two digit amounts. Make sure the children have access to equipment that will help them find totals, such as number lines, bead strings, writing materials or even calculators!

Transport

Cars and buses
Building blocks:

- Multiplying
- Dividing
- Recording

Moving on:

Laying the foundations

You will need:

Shoe boxes, resources to decorate them with, lots of play people, number cards from one to five

Main activity:

Begin by making some cars and buses with the children using shoe boxes. Perhaps they could stick on some wheels and windows. Work with four or five children and make sure each child has their own bus or car. Ask a child to turn over a number card. Challenge the children to put the correct number of people in their vehicle to match the card turned over. Can they find the matching numeral to put in their vehicle? Talk about whether everyone has collected the same number of passengers. This is good opportunity to develop counting skills and understanding of conservation as a collection of three passengers can be arranged in many different ways but still remains three passengers! Line up the vehicles in a pretend traffic jam and practice counting the repeated groups aloud. Then remove all passengers and repeat with different numbers. Children could also investigate sharing passengers between cars focusing on making sure groups are equal and fair. Any passengers who cannot fit in could be left at the bus stop! Children could record how many people were in each vehicle by drawing or taking photos. To support early addition and subtraction, simple stories could be told about passengers getting on and off the bus on a busy day to give children concrete experience of adding and subtracting as they add and remove passengers from their buses.

Make it easier: Focus on counting aloud, with the children initially, repeated groups of one and two in up to five or ten vehicles and sharing passengers fairly between two vehicles. To take this outside, children could ride on wheeled toys outside to make their own traffic jams, with an adult modelling counting aloud how many passengers are in the jam. Large boxes or mats could become buses and children could get themselves into groups of a given number on each bus, e.g. one, two, three or four passengers in each bus, with anyone left out going to the bus stop!

Make it harder: Following on from the body pattern activity, children could practice only saying the final person in each vehicle aloud, whilst another child records the numbers said aloud on a number square or track to highlight patterns. Children could also investigate which numbers of passengers can be shared equally between two, five or ten cars.

Transport

Parking fun!
Building blocks:

- Multiplying
- Dividing
- Recording

Moving on:

Building up

You will need:

Toy vehicles, shoe boxes to be garages, number cards from one to five, number line

Main activity:

Take on the role of a bossy parking attendant who decides how many vehicles can park in the garages each day. Working with a small group, either give children their own shoe box and group of ten toy cars, or put children in pairs to work. Hold up a number card and challenge the children to put that many vehicles in their garages (shoe boxes). Ask them to double check they have parked the correct number of vehicles and record the number on a sticky note which they then attach to the front of their box. Put the garages in a row and reinforce the fact that each garage has the same number, e.g. 'we have got four garages and each one has two cars in it; that is two and two and two and two: four lots of two'. Practice counting them altogether and challenge children to identify and perhaps circle the number on a number line or square. Remove the vehicles and choose another number. Repeat the activity, reinforcing the language outlined earlier and compare, did we have more or fewer cars altogether? How do you know? To explore sharing, children could investigate which numbers of cars can be shared fairly between two or more boxes, for example, by setting simple word problems such as 'There are ten cars that need to park and two/five/ten car parks. If we share the cars fairly, how many would park in each one?' Challenge children to explain how they could solve the problem. Provide paper or whiteboards for them to record their workings in their own ways, such as using pictures, symbols, tallies and so on.

Make it easier: Focus on making groups of the same size. Set out four or five car parks with a sticky note attached to each one with the same number on it, either one, two or three. Children take it in turns to roll a 'one, one, two, two, three, three' dice and after each throw have to collect the correct number of vehicles and decide which car parks to put them into with the aim being that in the end all of the car parks will have the correct number of cars in them. So if a three was rolled and each car park needed two, they could put two cars in one box and decide where to put the other. Once all the car parks have the correct number of cars inside them, practice counting how many altogether.

Make it harder: Give children pieces of card to be their garages and counters to be their vehicles. Each child has their own set of two, five or ten 'garages' (i.e. pieces of card) and pile of counters. They roll a 'one, one, two, two, three, three' dice which tells them how many cars (counters) to put in each garage (card). The children put the correct number of counters on each card, before counting the groups, e.g. 2 + 2 + 2 + 2 + 2. They record the correct number sentences to reflect this. For some children working securely and confidently at the 'building up' phase, the multiplication sign could be introduced as an alternative way of recording, e.g. 'We have four lots of two cars so we can write 4×2 as well as 2 + 2 + 2 + 2'.

Transport

Space jam
Building blocks:

- Multiplying
- Dividing
- Recording

Moving on:

Building up

You will need:

Large plastic building bricks, a wooden cube for making a dice and stickers, or one of the commercially produced large dices with pockets on each face for slipping pictures into, a one-to-six numbered dice, large plastic bricks, whiteboard pens

Main activity:

This would link well to a space or transport theme, and could be linked to stories about space. Tell the children that you are going to invent some different space vehicles together. One will have two wheels, one will have five wheels and one will have ten wheels. Once they have spent some time thinking of the vehicles, explain that they will be using these to play a game. Start by drawing the three vehicles they have designed on a dice, each vehicle will be on the dice twice. It would be easier to draw the vehicles onto stickers and then stick these onto a wooden cube, or use one of the large dice which has pockets for slipping pictures into on each face. Explain to the children that they will roll the two dice, to find out how many vehicles to put into their traffic jam. Each child rolls the two dice (numbered and pictured) and collects the correct number of bricks to represent the number rolled. Using a whiteboard pen they then add the correct number of wheels to each brick (by simply drawing large dots on the brick using the whiteboard pen) to match the type of vehicle rolled, e.g. either marking two, five or ten wheels on each brick depending on which type of transport was rolled, ensuring that all vehicles in their queue have the correct number of wheels. Challenge the children to record the correct number sentence to match their traffic jam (i.e. the number of wheels), for example if the number five dice was rolled, and the picture of the two-wheeled vehicle was rolled, there would be five vehicles with two wheels in the jam, and the number sentence $2 + 2 + 2 + 2 + 2 = 10$ would be recorded. Again for those children working securely the multiplication sign could be introduced as another way of recording a repeated addition number sentence. Children could either take it in turns to roll and make their own traffic jams, or the dice could be rolled in the middle of the group. If working individually, children could investigate whether a shorter traffic jam always has fewer wheels. For example, if two ten-wheeled vehicles were in a jam, how many two-wheeled or five-wheeled vehicles would be needed to make the same total number of wheels? Outside, large dice could be used and either cardboard boxes to represent the vehicles or large plastic bricks. Make sure the children only use whiteboard markers as these will erase easily from the bricks after the game. Putting the wheels on themselves, also provides a concrete experience of making, and counting, repeated groups. To turn this into a division activity, children could practice sharing a total of wheels (i.e. round counters with sticky tack on them) between a group of vehicles equally, to investigate which numbers can be shared equally between two, five or ten vehicles.

Make it easier: Children could make vehicles using construction toys such as bricks and blocks. Children roll a dice to find out how many wheels their vehicles have to have, i.e. two, two, three, three, four, four. All children within the small group make a vehicle with this number of wheels, then practice lining the vehicles up together and counting the repeated groups of wheels. To practice sharing, the children could share piles of wheels fairly between the group, ensuring everyone gets the same number to reinforce the idea of sharing fairly.

Make it harder: Children could progress onto drawing the vehicles and wheels, and use the 'x' sign to record the matching number sentences. Simple word problems could be given such as 'There were five vehicles in the space jam. Each one had five wheels, how many wheels was that altogether?' Children must be encouraged to share their ideas about how they could solve the problem and what to draw to find the answer. Also, for division, problems such as 'Altogether there were 20 wheels in the traffic jam. Each vehicle had five wheels. How many vehicles were there?' or for a more open problem: 'In the traffic jam there were ten wheels altogether. Each vehicle had the same number of wheels. How many vehicles were there?' Again encourage children to work practically to solve this, perhaps using wheels and bricks or by drawing.

Assessment and observation

- Do they respond to and use language related to addition and subtraction in play and everyday activities?
- Can they count objects to find out how many 'altogether'? Or count to find how many are 'left'?
- Do they make up their own problems to solve during play activities?
- Do they know any number facts by heart (e.g. doubles or bonds)?
- How do they record numbers or their thinking about calculation (e.g. pictures, tallies)?
- Can they talk about or show how they solved a problem?

? Stumbling blocks

The child is unable to count two groups altogether and counts them as two separate groups, e.g. 'one, two, three... one, two' when counting three and two more.

- Provide opportunities to count two groups as one, physically pushing the two groups together to make one large group. Model this clearly with the child pointing to the groups and saying, for example 'three add two equals...' then push the groups together to form a large group which he/she counts as one group.
- Provide lots of opportunities to practice counting aloud in different contexts, e.g. where children are in a line and some more join, or have toy cars in a traffic jam and more come along.
- Model counting two groups together with the child, with them pointing to the items and you counting aloud so that they hear you counting the groups together.
- Use actions such as jumping, clapping, stamping to reinforce counting, so the adult claps one, two, three, the child continues four, five, six, etc. This could be played as a group with each person adding to the claps.
- Play rolling and collecting games where the child rolls a dice and collects the correct number of items, then rolls again and adds more before counting altogether with adult modelling: 'you rolled three and then you rolled two... lets count altogether: one, two, three, four, five'. As the child progresses in this area and becomes secure at counting all items, move towards not needing to count the first group, but counting on instead: 'three... four, five'.
- Yoghurt pots with two sections are great for having two separate groups of small items, e.g. dried beans which are then combined as the corner is flipped over.

The child struggles to count on or back mentally, for example when asked to count on/back two from seven, the child says 'seven, one, two', instead of 'eight, nine' or 'six, five'.

- Encourage the child to put the starting number in their head, e.g. seven and put up two fingers to represent counting on/back two. As they tap their head they say 'seven', and then continue the count by putting down the two fingers as they say, 'eight, nine' or 'six, five'.
- Provide lots of counting aloud opportunities forwards and backwards starting from and finishing at different numbers, not just 1 to 10 or 20 but 13 to 17, or 22 to 13, etc., to reinforce children's knowledge of the number system.

The child always counts on or back, starting with the first number said, so is always one number out, e.g. when counting on two from seven, the child says 'seven, eight', not 'eight, nine'.

- Provide opportunities for lots of very active number line work. Make a large number line inside or out using chalk or masking tape on the carpet. Give children a starting number to stand on and as they jump forwards or back they begin their count.
- Ensure there are opportunities to play board games and use tracks where dice are rolled and the first move is the move forwards, not counting the space they are on.
- Provide smaller scale number line work with a small frog or animal jumping along a number line as the dice is rolled.

The child struggles to record number sentences, using incorrect symbols or putting them in the wrong place. (This relates to a child operating at the building up level, use of signs at earlier stages is not developmentally appropriate as the focus needs to be on concrete experiences and understanding, not mathematical symbols.)

- When working with the children develop some agreed actions for adding, subtracting and equals, such as forearms in a cross for adding, forearms parallel for equals, one forearm for subtracting. Use these together as you say number problems out loud, e.g. three 'add' four 'equals' seven with children acting out the signs as you say the problem. Children can be encouraged to record these correctly after saying them aloud.
- Help children to understand that the equals sign means 'is the same as', if using physical gestures for equals, pointing your forefingers to emphasis this balance. Encourage children to say 'is the same as' as they record number sentences to help them put = in the correct place, e.g. '2 + 3 is the same as...'. This will help them as they progress when = is not always in the same place!

The child chooses the wrong operation to solve simple word problems.

- Even with young children when you solve simple problems ask them 'Am I getting more or will I have less?' to help them develop an understanding of how to interpret a simple problem.
- Take time working with children to share some simple word problems and talk about the language in them. Older children and able readers could underline the words they think tell them what to do: 'altogether', 'left', and so on.
- Make word banks of adding, subtraction, multiplication and division words (as appropriate) with the children and display these and refer to these when problem solving. It is so much more relevant and holds more value for the children when they are involved in making these types of word banks. The children will be much more likely to refer to these than the almost wallpaper type resources often printed out from websites.
- Look at some simple problems with the children (do not focus on solving them) and sort them into addition and subtraction problems (this could also be done with multiplication and division problems for children beyond the stages identified). How do they know whether to add/subtract? Can they record a number sentence to match the problem?
- Make up some word problems together, painting, drawing or taking pictures to accompany them for a display.
- Have some picture cards of items related to your current theme and some + and – cards. Children turn over an object card, e.g. transport, and an operation card '–' and have to think of a subtraction word problem about the picture selected.

⚒ Useful tools

Counting objects (caution to be taken with small children handling small objects)
Empty chocolate boxes, yoghurt pots with sections/tubs
Number lines
Number tracks
Number squares
Money (real pennies if possible!)
Bead strings
Number cards
Hoops
Paper plates
Chalks
Pens

Clipboards
Dice
Simple board or track games
Repeated sets/pairs of objects: wellies, socks, animals, cups and saucers, knives, forks and spoons and so on
Number rhyme puppets and props

Stories and rhymes

Stories

Just Like Jasper by Nick Butterworth and Mick Inkpen, 2008, Hodder Children's Books.
I Went to the Zoopermarket by Nick Sharratt, 2006, Scholastic.
Bumper to Bumper: A Traffic Jam by Jakki Wood, 1996, Simon and Schuster.
The Shopping Basket by John Burningham, 1992, Red Fox.
Aliens Love Underpants by Claire Freedman, 2007, Simon and Schuster.

Rhymes

Make them harder by having not just one coming or going! Remember you do not always have to start with ten or five!
'Ten in the bed'
'Ten green bottles'
'One elephant went out to play…'
'Five fat sausages'
'The animals went in two by two'
'Five little speckled frogs'
'Five little monkeys jumping on the bed'

5 | Shape and space

Introduction

Shapes and patterns can be found all around us, particularly in nature, from the rings on an old tree trunk to the spiral on a snail's shell. Opening children's eyes to these provides an invaluable beginning to their appreciation and understanding of pattern, which is inherent in all areas of mathematics. Number and calculating is built upon patterns, for example recognising sequences of numbers or the shape of five on dice with spots, without counting each dot. Throughout children's early years they will have begun to make connections between shapes and familiar aspects of the world, such as the round wheels on their family car or the shape and size of the box or packet of their favourite treats. Children are noticing these shapes; however, the importance of talking about them is paramount if they are to develop the language to describe the shapes and patterns that they see. This is just as true for position and direction, modelling and giving clear instructions to children to develop the breadth of vocabulary will ensure they too can communicate their thinking effectively.

Figure 5.1 Playing with and exploring shapes lays the foundations for a
solid understanding of the properties of shapes.

Everyday experiences of shape and space

- Instructions to complete simple tasks
- Directions to locate objects in the home or when out and about
- Shapes of containers, boxes and pots
- Features of houses, such as windows, doors, fences, gates
- Patterns in nature, such as trees, leaves, insects, clouds, flowers
- Shape sorter toys
- Building bricks
- Jigsaws and puzzles
- Remote control cars
- Road signs and markings
- Train track and roadway toys

What are the building blocks?

Naming and describing 2D and 3D shapes

This is about children learning to recognise, name and talk about flat and solid shapes within their learning environment and everyday lives. The mathematical language used to describe the properties of 2D and 3D shapes is often challenging for children. However, if this language is used by adults alongside their everyday vocabulary from a young age, children will begin to recognise, visualise and describe these shapes with much greater ease.

Pattern

This is about recognising, copying and creating patterns using shapes, colours and objects. Being able to identify and create patterns is a key aspect of mathematics as pattern is inherent in number, calculating and problem solving.

Position

This is about children describing where an object or person is in relation to something else using positional language.

Direction and movement

This is about using everyday and mathematical language to give instructions, describing how something moves and in which direction it is travelling. This can be in relation to a person, object or something requiring instructions, such as a programmable toy.

💬 Key vocabulary

- Names for 2D shapes: circle, square, triangle, rectangle, hexagon, octagon, pentagon
- Names for 3D shapes: cube, cuboid, pyramid, cone, cylinder, sphere, triangular prism, square-based pyramid
- Curved
- Flat
- Solid
- Round
- Corner
- Edge
- Face
- Side
- Roll
- Slide
- Position
- Direction
- Forwards
- Backwards
- Turn
- Left
- Right
- Clockwise
- Anticlockwise
- Above
- Below
- Next to
- On top
- Behind
- Between
- After
- Before
- Under
- In front of

Moving on:
What does it look like at the three stages of progression?

Laying the foundations
Children at this stage:

- show an interest in shape and space by playing with shapes or making arrangements with objects;
- show an awareness of similarities of shapes in the environment;
- use positional language;
- show an interest in shape by sustained construction activity or by talking about shapes or arrangements;
- show an interest in shapes in the environment;
- use shapes appropriately for tasks;
- begin to talk about the shapes of everyday objects, e.g. 'round' and 'tall'.

Beginning to build
Children at this stage:

- begin to use mathematical names for 'solid' 3D shapes and 'flat' 2D shapes, and mathematical terms to describe shapes;
- can select a particular named shape;
- can describe their relative position, such as 'behind' or 'next to';
- use familiar objects and common shapes to create and recreate patterns and build models;
- recognise, create and describe patterns;
- explore characteristics of everyday objects and shapes and use mathematical language to describe them.

Building up

Children at this stage:

- visualise and name common 2D shapes and 3D solids and describe their features;
- use shapes to make patterns, pictures and models;
- identify objects that turn about a point (e.g. scissors) or about a line (e.g. a door) and recognise and make whole, half and quarter turns;
- visualise and use everyday language to describe the position of objects and direction and distance when moving them, for example when placing or moving objects on a game board.

Building together

 Out and about

Patterns, patterns everywhere
Building blocks:

- Describing properties of shapes
- Pattern

Moving on:

Laying the foundations

You will need:

Pipe cleaners, straws, camera, wheels, bricks, boxes, tubes, etc.

Main activity:

Talk to the children about how they find out about the world around them and the importance of their eyes. Discuss how to make good observations of their world; look very carefully, then talk about what they see. Explain that they are going to look for shapes that are all around them, but to help them look carefully they will wear magic shape glasses. Children make a pair of glasses using pipe cleaners or straws and decorate them. Children put their magic glasses on and then start hunting around the indoor and outdoor area to find shapes. Draw the children's attention to shapes within nature, such as on tree trunks, snail shells, leaves and clouds, as well as man-made objects, such as buildings and structures. How could they describe the shapes and patterns they observe? Help the children to record their findings by photographing the children alongside the objects. Encourage the children to talk about the shapes they have spotted using their own words and everyday language. Model the correct mathematical language to describe the same properties such as 'curved', 'straight' and 'round' and name shapes if they are unknown to the child. Print the photos and then compare the everyday objects; are any of the photographed objects the same shape as each other? How are they different? Can they make labels or captions with an adult to accompany their photos to describe the shapes or patterns they can see?

Make it easier: Provide children with the opportunity to look at objects, or pictures of objects that have very obvious shapes or shape properties, such as bricks, windows, wheels, etc. Encourage children to explore language to describe them in their own way. Model appropriate mathematical words to support their understanding and enable them to verbalise what they can see.

Make it harder: Encourage a multi-sensory approach to finding out more about the shapes of everyday objects by providing children with objects such as different sized wheels, bricks, boxes, tubes, etc. and give them time to explore what they can do with them. For example, can they roll them? Build with them? Model mathematical vocabulary for the children whilst they are talking about what they have found out, such as 'it can roll because this part of it is curved' or 'you can stack the boxes because the tops and bottoms of them are flat'. Introduce the names of flat 2D and solid 3D shapes as appropriate when talking with the children.

Out and about

Shapes in nature
Building blocks:

- Describing properties of shapes

Moving on:

Beginning to build

You will need:

Stones, sticks, twigs, pebbles, bamboo canes, camera

Main activity:

Children or adults should collect stones, pebbles, sticks and twigs from around the outdoor area and place them in a large tray. Look around the outdoor area, can the children spot any shapes? Can they name them? Can they talk about the shapes they can see and describe any of their properties? Explain that they will be using natural resources to create 2D shapes. Can they think of a shape and describe it? Listen to the children, and model the use of mathematical language such as 'sides', 'corners', 'round' and 'straight' if they describe the shape using everyday language. Allow children time to choose and use the natural resources to make a 2D shape. Ask children to talk about how they have arranged the resources and what they can tell you about the shape they have made. Support children with checking properties of 2D shapes, such as whether the shape has the correct number of corners and sides. Take photographs of the shapes they have created. Print the photos and enlarge them, children can then label their own and others' photographs with sticky labels to describe the properties of the shapes.

Make it easier: Provide the children with the natural resources and allow them time to play with these, creating arrangements and shapes. Talk to them about what they are doing, and discuss any shapes that they make during their play. Model how to make simple shapes such as circles using stones or pebbles. Can they copy this using the resources available?

Make it harder: Provide children with bamboo canes or strong, long sticks. Explain that they are going to use the canes/sticks to create a square-based pyramid. What do the children know about the properties of a pyramid which will help them decide how to arrange the sticks? Talk about the number of faces and corners with the children and allow them time looking at pyramids to ensure they can visualise the shape they are to produce. Children then 'build' a pyramid and check their work with a partner. Are there any other 3D shapes that they could create with the canes/sticks?

Out and about

Building patterns

Building blocks:

- Describing properties of shapes

Moving on:

Building up

You will need:

Crayons, paper, 3D shapes, barriers (such as large hardback books), camera, clipboards, and pencils

Main activity:

Take a walk around the local area or outdoor space and look for shapes together. Talk about the shapes they can see on buildings or houses. Are the shapes they can see flat or solid? Look carefully at the bricks on a building or house. Make rubbings of walls using paper and wax crayons. Ask them to talk about the shapes and patterns they have created. Explain that bricks are not flat like the rubbings they have taken; they are cuboids with rectangular faces. Discuss other features of buildings and the 3D shapes that they can see, such as a cuboid chimney, cylindrical fence posts, triangular prism roof and cuboid letter box. Ask children to record these shapes using their own drawings with paper and clipboards to help them when they are building their own houses using shapes. Children could also take photographs of the shapes they can see using the zoom feature on a camera and print these to support their construction work. Once back inside, provide children with a range of 3D shapes, ensuring that there are a variety of each shape, such as long and thin cuboids as well as regular cuboids. Ask children to design their own house or building using a picture and to label the shapes they are going to use. Children then work with a partner with a barrier between them. One describes their design to the other, explaining which shapes to choose and where to place them. Once their partner has completed the building the barrier is then removed and they can check whether the correct shapes have been used.

Make it easier: Use the same activity but instead focus on 2D shapes that can be seen in the outdoor environment and only provide 2D shapes to create pictures of houses and buildings rather than models.

Make it harder: When in the outdoor area focus children's attention on the properties of the shapes that they can see, such as the curved face of a fence post. When children complete drawings of the buildings, encourage them to label shapes with the properties they know about them. Once inside, repeat the same barrier game but instead of naming the shapes for their partner to use ask children to describe the shape, for example 'This shape has six square faces and eight corners. It is on top of the cuboid'.

Puzzles and games

Gone fishing

Building blocks:

- Recognising shapes

Moving on:

Laying the foundations

You will need:

Floating toys, fishing rods/nets, coloured buckets, 2D shape labels, waterproof markers, laminated card

Main activity:

This game has the same principle as a shape sorter toy that toddlers and small children enjoy exploring. Using a set of floating toys such as ducks or boats, label each with a laminated picture of a shape. Explain to the children that they will use the fishing rods/nets to catch an item. But once they have caught one it needs to be sorted into the correct bucket. Use four different coloured buckets, each labelled with a common 2D shape for children to match their shapes to and place them in the corresponding bucket. Encourage the children to name the shapes as they catch them and talk to them about the shapes using everyday language. Once all of the toys have been caught can the children count how many are in each bucket? Which has the most/least? Set challenges for children such as 'Who can catch the most circles/round shapes?' Once children have completed the game give them an opportunity to create their own version by labelling floating toys with their own shapes or patterns. Provide them with waterproof markers and pieces of laminated card to draw on and then stick them on the toys. Repeat the game and encourage them to talk with their friends about the shapes and patterns as they catch the toys together.

Make it easier: Have only two shapes to choose from so that they are distinguishing only between two shapes that have different properties, such as a square and a circle. Name the shapes as they are caught and encourage the child to copy you as they place the shape in the bucket.

Make it harder: Change the pictures on the buckets to represent the properties of the shapes, for example four straight lines could be drawn and numbered for all shapes with four sides to be put in that bucket or a picture of a corner on one bucket then the same picture crossed out on another bucket to show sorting into 'corners' and 'no corners'. The children could then work together to make their own labels for the buckets.

 ## Puzzles and games

Bingo
Building blocks:

- Recognising shapes

Moving on:

Beginning to build

You will need:

Blank squared paper for bingo boards, a variety of different sized 2D shapes, bag

Main activity:

Give children or pairs of children large squared paper with a 3 × 2 area. Explain that they are going to create their own bingo boards. Provide trays of different sized 2D shapes for them to choose from and then place six shapes on their board, one in each square. Can they name the shapes they have chosen for their board? Ensure that all children are given access to familiar shapes but those that need a further challenge have the opportunity to use less familiar shapes such as a hexagon or irregular shapes such as a scalene triangle. Model being the bingo caller by placing all possible shapes in a bag then, taking one shape at a time, call the name and size of the shape to the children. This can be done by calling the name whilst the shape is still in the bag. Remind the children that whatever the orientation or if they are regular or irregular shapes they are still known by the same name. If children have that shape on their boards they can remove it. Show the children the shape to enable them to check they have removed the correct one. The first child to remove all their shapes shouts 'bingo'. Once modelled, children can take turns as the bingo caller. Encourage the use of correct language to name and describe the shape. This game could then be repeated using familiar 3D shapes.

Make it easier: Only provide children with a three section bingo board and regular 2D shapes (circle, square, rectangle and triangle) to choose from. When calling the names of the shape ensure the children can see the shape at the same time as the name is being called so that they can associate the name with the shape and check their boards.

Make it harder: Instead of calling the names of the shapes use the properties for a 'What am I?' clue. For example, instead of calling 'square' you could use the clue 'I have four straight sides that are all the same length and four corners'. Ensure the language used includes correct mathematical terms. Children can then take on the role of caller. Observe and support their use of language to describe the shapes. For example, if they choose to describe the corners as 'points' model the use of the term 'corners' using the same sentence.

Puzzles and games

Headbands

Building blocks:

- Recognising shapes
- Describing properties of shapes

Moving on:

Building up

You will need:

3D shapes, paper headbands, 3D shape pictures, 2D shapes and pictures of them

Main activity:

Provide a small group with a set of 3D shapes (cylinder, sphere, cube, cuboid, pyramid, prism, cone) and a pack of pictures of the same 3D shapes. Each child also needs a headband made from a ring of paper. Explain that the game will involve a picture of a 3D shape being fixed onto their headband without them seeing and they can ask questions to guess the shape but the only answers the rest of the group can give are 'yes' or 'no'. Look at the shapes together. Can the children name all of them? Also talk about the language they could use to describe each shape and record key vocabulary on a board or on paper for children to see, such as 'faces', 'edges' and 'corners'. One child then leaves the group and the rest of the children decide which shape they will choose to place on the missing child's headband. When the child returns stick the picture onto their headband without them seeing. They can then ask questions to find out which shape they have on their headband. Support the child by rephrasing questions and using the correct language. The group then responds with 'yes' or 'no'. After three or more questions they can then make a guess by looking at the shapes provided and thinking about their clues. The picture can then be revealed to show whether they are right or wrong. Children then take turns to be the one leaving the group and guessing. The game could also be played where the group give clues to the child wearing the headband and after every child has given a clue the child with the headband could then guess which shape they have.

Make it easier: Use 2D instead of 3D shapes as these shapes are more familiar to the children and the language is simpler. If 3D shapes were being used a smaller set could be offered that all have very different properties such as a cone, cube and sphere.

Make it harder: Limit the number of questions the child can ask so that they have to think carefully about the choice of language to get as much information as possible. A wider range of shapes could also be used by introducing a triangular prism and a triangular-based pyramid.

Celebrations

Wrapping presents
Building blocks:

- Pattern

Moving on:

Laying the foundations

You will need:

Junk modelling boxes, wrapping paper, counters/stones/buttons, picture books containing patterns, paper, paint, printing equipment

Main activity:

Use the context of a celebration to introduce this activity – birthdays, Christmas, Diwali, Hanukkah, etc. Explain that they will be wrapping presents (a range of junk modelling boxes) for the celebration. Provide a range of different wrapping paper, containing patterns of different pictures or shapes. Ask the children to describe the paper they are using. What do they notice? Is their wrapping paper that they have chosen the same as a friend's? How is it different? Talk about patterns on the wrapping paper – the repetition of the same pictures of shapes across the paper. Can they spot the patterns? Choose a different piece of wrapping paper and talk about whether the pattern on this paper is the same as the last piece or different. Can they place a counter/stone/button, etc. on all the pictures/shapes that are the same and then repeat with the other pictures/shapes? What do they notice? Say the patterns out loud together, such as 'clown, balloon, clown, balloon', and encourage children to continue talking about the pattern themselves.

Make it easier: Look at picture books together that contain patterns, such as shapes or lines. Talk about what they can see. Can they describe the patterns? Trace the patterns with their fingers whilst describing the patterns together. Share other stories including wild animals such as zebras, cheetahs, giraffes and snakes. Look at the patterns on their bodies and talk about the colours and what they can see. Are all the patterns the same? How are they different? Where else have they seen these sorts of patterns? Move on from looking at pictures to looking at the objects around them such as their clothes. Do they spot any patterns on their clothes, such as on their socks, jumpers or tights?

Make it harder: Give children blank pieces of wrapping paper and paint with printing equipment. Can they create their own wrapping paper? Once they have attempted this, talk about what they have done. Have they used any patterns on their paper? Can they talk about them? If they have not used patterns on their paper, work together to add patterns by repeating pictures or shapes (use a simple ABAB pattern across the paper). Talk about the pattern out loud together until children can continue this independently.

 ## Celebrations

Paper chains
Building blocks:

- Pattern

Moving on:

Beginning to build

You will need:

Coloured paper strips

Main activity:

Explain that the children are in charge of decorating the room for a celebration by making paper chains (this could be linked to celebrations such as Chinese New Year, Christmas or birthdays, during which houses are decorated as part of the celebration). Get a box of paper strips out to show them what they can use. Provide paper of two different colours. Talk to them about how they could use these to decorate the room. Use the coloured paper strips to create a paper chain in an ABAB pattern. What do the children notice about the way you have arranged the coloured strips? Can they talk about what they see and do they know which colour strip would be used next in the chain? How do they know? Ask children to help you to continue the pattern and use language such as 'pattern' and 'repeating' to describe what you are doing together. Children could then use their own coloured strips to explore pattern. Can they recreate a similar pattern as the one demonstrated but using two different colours? Can they talk about how they recreated the pattern; how did they know which order to put the colours in? Try to challenge the children to move beyond ABAB patterns. What if they had three colours, what could the pattern look like then? Can they describe the pattern they have used for their chain to a friend? Can their friend continue the pattern to make the chain longer?

Make it easier: Encourage children to use the same colours as you modelled to create the same pattern on their chains. Can they say the pattern aloud as they are making the chain? If this is challenging, get the children to work in pairs with each child being responsible for one colour. They can then work together to make the chain by taking turns to add their colour to the chain to create the repeating pattern.

Make it harder: Provide children with three different coloured paper strips and ask them to investigate how many different repeating patterns they can make using those three colours, if they are allowed to use each colour more than once, for example red, blue, green or red, red, green etc. How will they know when they have found all the different possibilities for three colours? Encourage them to check with a friend to ensure they have not forgotten any combinations. What if they had four colours? Could they predict how many different pattern chains they could make now? Children work together to make different patterns using four colours and then ask them to count how many different patterns they could make. How will they know when they have found all the different possibilities?

Celebrations

Birthday colours
Building blocks:

● Pattern

Moving on:

Building up

You will need:

Blue and red paper for each child, red and blue pens, red and blue cubes, a puppet

Main activity:

Introduce the children to a puppet and explain that he is about to celebrate a birthday and has two favourite colours: red and blue. He is going to be five years old. When he was one he had red balloons and red icing on his cake. When he was two he had blue balloons and blue icing on his cake. This pattern continued each year; one year everything was red and the next year everything was blue. What colour will his balloons and icing be for his birthday this year now he is turning five? Talk about methods for working out which colour will be the fifth. Discuss children's ideas and prompt them to think about whether drawing pictures or making jottings would help them to work out the answer. Allow time for children to make their predictions. Have sheets of blue and red paper for children to choose to show their answer. Children to hold up the colour they think will be used for the puppet's fifth birthday. How did they know? Can they explain their reasoning? Write the numbers to represent each birthday (one, two, three, etc.) in the correct colours, i.e. red or blue. Do the children notice a pattern? What do they notice about all the numbers that are red/blue? Talk about the pattern emerging and use this to check the answer for the fifth colour. Discuss the idea of odd and even numbers linked to the pattern. Using what they have found out, can they predict what colour his tenth birthday might be? The fifteenth? How could they check their answers? Demonstrate using coloured numbers or the odd/even pattern to check together.

Make it easier: Make coloured number lines, using red and blue for alternate numbers, and use coloured cubes to make towers to represent each age to form a staircase to show the pattern in visual ways. When predicting, ask the children to guess which colour the following age from the last one modelled would be so that they can rely more on using the repeating pattern rather than the notion of odd and even numbers.

Make it harder: Give children the opportunity to develop their reasoning skills by posing questions such as 'The puppet thinks that there will be blue balloons and blue icing on his cake on his eighteenth birthday. Do you agree?' Encourage children to not only explain their thinking orally but ask them to demonstrate how they know using pictures, apparatus or diagrams.

 ## Journeys

Train ride

Building blocks:

- Position
- Direction and movement

Moving on:

Laying the foundations

You will need:

Small teddies or play people, wooden or plastic train track with train carriages, large paper, junk modelling resources, card, crayons, felt tips, chalk

Main activity:

Explain to the children that you are going to take some passengers (teddies, play people, etc.) on a train ride. Show them the box of train track and ask if anyone knows how to start building a track. Do they want to have a long straight track or a circular track? Encourage children to think carefully about the pieces of track they are choosing and talk to them about how to use them to construct the track together. Once the track has been made count the passengers into the carriages and talk about ideas of what they might see on their train journey. Record these ideas on a large piece of paper and then use resources such as coloured paper, junk modelling and card to make some of the suggested features, for example a pond, bridge, tunnel or trees. Place the features around the train track with the children; which will they see first on their journey? What will they see after that? After the features have been added to the track use the train to go on a journey. Model talking about the journey as the train travels, for example 'the train goes over the bridge, next to the lake and then through the tunnel'. Use positional language as you talk about the train and encourage the children to copy the words you are using. Let the children play with the train track and pose questions such as 'Where is the train going now?' to prompt children to talk about the journey. The features can be changed around so that new journeys can be discussed and further features can also be added to extend the use of vocabulary such as 'under', 'over', 'through', 'next to', 'behind'. It is important for children not only to have their own turn talking through a journey but to also listen to an adult and other children talking as this will develop their vocabulary and listening skills.

Make it easier: Create a group train journey using the track. Each time the train comes to a feature on the track compose a sentence together to describe what it is doing and then repeat this several times together, such as 'over the bridge, over the bridge, over the bridge' using the rhythm of a train in your voice. Repeat this for each feature and then encourage the children to take the train on its journey and say each phrase as it travels around the track.

Make it harder: Once children have explored different journeys using the train track, provide them with large pieces of paper with crayons or felt tips or chalk in an outdoor area and ask them to make a large map of their own train journey. Children can then walk on the map (if in the outdoor area) or use toy trains to tell a friend or adult about the journey. Listen for the use of positional language and model or rephrase the correct vocabulary as appropriate. What if they were then going on a car journey? Or a journey in a hot air balloon? Can they make a new map with features of what they would see on this new journey and talk through their journey to an adult? Again, observe their use of language and introduce new words such as 'above' and 'below' in the hot air balloon journey.

Journeys

Treasure hunt

Building blocks:

- Position
- Direction and movement

Moving on:

Beginning to build

You will need:

A picture or photo of a teddy/puppet, written clues using positional/directional language, a teddy/puppet

Main activity:

Show children a picture or photo of a teddy or puppet that is familiar to the children and explain that he is lost somewhere within the setting. How could they find him? Introduce the idea that there are a number of clues that will lead them to the lost teddy if they follow them carefully. Create a treasure hunt of clues for the children to follow around the indoor or outdoor environment. Use positional and directional language within the clues to prompt discussion during the hunt. These could include the direction and rough number of steps to take to the area where the next clue is hidden and then more detail about where the clue is using positional language. For example a clue may say 'Take ten giant steps forwards. The next clue is under the flower pot' or 'Look behind you and face the fence. Now walk forwards. The next clue is on top of the fence post at the left end of the fence'. When the clues are being read aloud highlight the positional and directional language. Can the children use this language to locate the next clue? Observe their movements when following each clue. At the end of the final clue children will find the lost teddy.

Make it easier: Have one clue to find the lost teddy such as 'It is on top of the swing' or 'It is under the bush'. Talk to the children about where the clue is telling them to look and emphasise the positional language within the clues. Children can then take turns hiding the teddy and give a friend or adult a clue about where the teddy is. Encourage them to use similar positional language as in the previous clues rather than saying 'It's over there'.

Make it harder: Allow children to work together to create their own clues for a new location to find the lost teddy. Support them in deciding where the teddy will be hidden and begin with the clue that leads others to this spot, then write a clue to describe where the final clue will be hidden and so on. An adult could scribe for the children and note any directional or positional language that they use. If their wording could be rephrased to use positional or directional language, model the new clue aloud or work as a team to refine the language within clues. Other children from the setting can then follow the clues to locate the teddy and evaluate how clear and easy the clues were to follow.

Journeys

Pathways
Building blocks:

- Position,
- Direction and movement

Moving on:

Building up

You will need:

Rubber spots/arrows, blindfolds, apparatus such as benches, mats and tables, musical instruments, a programmable toy

Main activity:

Talk about things in the children's experience that turn. When do we turn when we are walking or travelling? Practise making whole and half turns when moving around an open space. Introduce the concept of a quarter turn to the right (clockwise) and the left (anticlockwise). Explain that when we are walking in the local area we use quarter turns to turn corners. Provide children with a number of large rubber spots or arrows that can be placed or stuck on the floor. Explain that they are going to create a pathway between two points using the markers and that they will work in pairs, where one will be blindfolded and the other will direct them along the pathway without touching them. Set the markers out with opportunities for children to make ninety degree turns to move around corners. Model how to give clues that include the number of steps to take and the direction to turn to travel in the correct direction. Highlight the vocabulary that determines direction or movement such as 'quarter turn', 'left', 'right', 'forwards' and 'three steps forwards'. One child in the pair is blindfolded and guided to the starting marker. Their partner stands alongside them and is allowed to speak to them but not touch them (unless a potential hazard is ahead). Listen to the language the children use to guide their friend. Praise the use of correct mathematical language and rephrase any instructions that could be made clearer by using the vocabulary discussed with the group. When children have completed the task talk to them about how easy it was to give and follow instructions. Are there any words that they or their partners used to make it easier?

Make it easier: Set out equipment such as benches, mats and tables in an open space. Explain that the children are going to practise turns whilst walking along or jumping off the apparatus or across the floor or mats. Show two instruments with contrasting sounds, such as a tambourine and a drum. Each time the tambourine is shaken children need to freeze and then complete a whole turn; this can be by jumping or simply turning on the spot, depending on which apparatus they are on. When the drum is beaten the children must instead perform a half turn. The children should move freely around the space and turn as instructed by the instrument. Ask the children to demonstrate their turns and continue to model the language 'whole turn' and 'half turn' as they perform.

Make it harder: Encourage children to use the words 'clockwise' and 'anticlockwise' instead of 'left' and 'right' when describing turns. Once they have been able to successfully direct a friend along the pathway suggest they create their own pathways to use with a programmable toy. Can they record their instructions for the toy using words or symbols, such as F for forwards or TR for turn right. They could also use arrows to show the commands 'turn' or 'forwards' and the number of units the toy will move forwards next to the arrow. They can then try programming these instructions into the toy and see if it reaches the correct destination.

Assessment and observation

- What shapes do they recognise in their learning environment?
- What words do they use to describe or talk about shapes and patterns?
- Can they use everyday or mathematical language to describe where something is?
- Can they use everyday or mathematical language to describe how to travel to a specific location?
- Can they talk about, copy and create patterns?

? Stumbling blocks

The child only recognises a square or triangle in its regular form.

- When setting up shape activities, ensure that there is a mix of regular and irregular shapes for children to explore and use.
- Play games such as 'Up the wall' where shapes are revealed gradually and guessed by children. Use these games to highlight properties of shapes, for example that a triangle has three sides and corners and show that this is true for all types of triangles.
- Use activities such as construction straws or peg boards with elastic bands for children to create their own variations of familiar shapes, challenge them to make as many different triangles, squares, etc. as possible.

The child is confused by the language used to describe shapes' properties such as 'faces' or 'sides'.

- Model the correct mathematical language when talking about shapes with children both in their play and during adult led tasks.
- Talk about how words can have different meanings, for example 'face' can relate to our faces with eyes, ears and noses and also the flat surface of a 3D shape. Draw faces on each surface of a cube to remind children the mathematical name for 3D shape properties.
- Make lists of mathematical words that have other meanings in children's lives, such as 'face', 'side', 'corner', 'take away'. Talk about these with the children and discuss how to use these correctly when talking about numbers and shapes.
- Establish the difference between 'side' and 'face' by constructing 2D and 3D shapes using construction straws, card, playdough, etc. Show that 'side' is only used to describe properties of flat shapes compared to 'face' describing properties of a solid shape.

The child states 'there' as their only description for where an object is, and is therefore unsure of how to use positional language effectively.

- Model positional language during everyday familiar tasks and ensure that instructions given to children include a range of language, such as 'Please can you get the scissors, they are behind the pencils?', rather than 'Please can you get the scissors, they are over there?'.
- Provide opportunities for children to take part in and set up treasure hunts using positional language within clues. Encourage children to be as accurate as possible and to choose the best positional vocabulary to describe the position of the treasure rather than just the words they are familiar with.
- Read stories that include a range of positional language and create your own version, such as *Rosie's Walk* or *We're Going on a Bear Hunt*.

Useful tools

A range of paper, plastic or wooden 2D and 3D shapes
Pictures of 2D and 3D shapes in a variety of orientations and sizes
Construction straws and equipment to build shapes
Pattern cards
Sorting circles and trays
Shape pictures for matching or filling
Peg boards and elastic bands
Apparatus such as benches, mats, tables, cones, markers
Train track, roadway
Small world people, teddies
Squared and dotty paper
Junk modelling containers in a range of shapes
Programmable toys
Patterned wrapping paper
Printing sponges and paint

Stories and rhymes

Stories

Rosie's Walk by Pat Hutchins, 2003, Red Fox.
The Shopping Basket by John Burningham, 1992, Red Fox.
We're Going on a Bear Hunt by Helen Oxenbury, 1997, Walker Books.

My Cat Likes to Hide in Boxes by Eve Sutton, 1978, Picture Puffin Books.
Kipper's Birthday by Mick Inkpen, 2008, Hodder, Children's Books.
The Train Ride by June Crebbin, 1997, Walker Books.
Oi! Get off Our Train by John Burningham, 1991, Red Fox.
The Patchwork Quilt by Valerie Flournoy, 1995, Picture Puffin Books.

Rhymes

'Twinkle twinkle'
'Hey diddle diddle'
'Jack and Jill'
'The grand old Duke of York'

6 All aboard: Building links and working with families

Over the years there has been a wide range of research conducted to establish the impact of parental involvement on children's learning. A key finding in *The Impact of Parental Involvement on Children's Education* (DCSF, 2008) confirmed that 'Parental involvement in children's education from an early age has a significant effect on educational achievement'. However, when talking about getting parents involved with children's mathematical learning there can be a number of challenges. Most parents feel confident about supporting their child's developing literacy skills through regular reading and writing activities. On the other hand, where maths is concerned many parents do not feel so confident. This can be caused in part by their own negative experiences of maths education or the fact that the methods taught today are very different to those taught during their own education resulting in a fear that they may teach their child incorrectly.

Figure 6.1 Inviting parents to join in with the typical types of activities that happen each and every day in schools and settings, can be a powerful way of highlighting the maths-rich potential of children's natural play and exploration.

It is the practitioners' job to help parents and carers to become more informed about how children learn maths and how vital their role is in supporting mathematical learning at home in fun, practical ways that do not require a work book. To enable parents to feel more confident and positive about supporting maths at home practitioners need to show parents that the everyday activities they are already enjoying with their child are full of real life maths. Although parents are already sharing these experiences with their children they may need further support to make the most of mathematical opportunities through questioning or modelling mathematical language.

Here are some simple ideas you could try in your setting to get parents engaged in mathematical learning.

Maths at home workshop

- Work with parents to brainstorm ideas for mathematical opportunities in everyday experiences, such as bath time, dinner time, at the shops, in the garden, cooking and journeys.
- Use their ideas to create a leaflet or booklet for other parents to use outlining simple activities that could take place, highlighting key language and questions. Highlight the importance of talking with your child and the modelling of correct mathematical language during play.
- Celebrate maths at home by building a display of photos based on the activities in the booklet and note any impact this has on their mathematical learning within the setting.

Mathematical learning at school/setting

- Brainstorm parents' feelings and ideas about maths. Be prepared that these could be quite negative and be sensitive towards this.
- Show photos of children engaged in continuous provision activities such as playdough, sand, water, role play and in the garden. Talk about the maths that is happening within this play.
- Invite parents to visit the setting and engage in activities with their children with a maths focus such as scoring games outside, cooking and board games.
- Revisit the initial brainstorm of feelings about maths and add any new comments to this in a different colour to highlight how parents viewed maths before the session and after playing with their children.

Games libraries

- Build up a collection of mathematical resources such as simple games, puzzles, dominoes and playing cards for parents to borrow to share with their children.

Number rhymes and songs

- Type up some rhymes in large text and send these home for parents to learn with their children. Practise these together in the setting using actions and props.

Story sacks

- Work with parents to develop some sacks linked to counting stories and number rhymes.
- Arrange a group of story sack makers to create sacks, or alternatively host a session where parents, children and practitioners work together to make sacks for favourite mathematical stories.

Maths packs

- Set up packs consisting of basic mathematical equipment such as dominoes, dice, counters, playing cards, number cards, number lines and whiteboards.
- Provide each family with a pack and set simple challenges to complete each week, promoting the use of the contents in a fun, practical way.

Through engaging parents in these types of activities the subject of maths can become demystified and, in turn, parents will begin to feel more confident about supporting their child's individual mathematical learning journey.

Bibliography

Cotton, T. (2010) *Understanding and Teaching Primary Mathematics*. Essex: Pearson Education Ltd

DCSF (2008) *The Impact of Parental Involvement on Children's Education*. Nottingham: DCSF Publications

Department for Education (2013) National Curriculum In England, Framework Document. www.education.gov.uk

Department for Education (2013) Early Years Outcomes. www.education.gov.uk

DfES (2006) *Primary Framework for Literacy and Mathematics*. London: DfES Publications

Early Education (2012) *Development Matters in the Early Years Foundation Stage (EYFS)*. London: Early Education

National Strategies (2008) *Mathematical Vocabulary Book*. London: National Strategies